THE HOUSEHOLD BOOK OF HINTS AND TIPS

THE HOUSEHOLD BOOK OF HINTS AND TIPS

DIANE RAINTREE

Illustrations By Susan Moskowitz

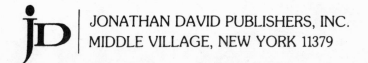

JONATHAN DAVID PUBLISHERS, INC.
MIDDLE VILLAGE, NEW YORK 11379

THE HOUSEHOLD BOOK
OF
HINTS AND TIPS
by
Diane Raintree

Copyright © 1979
by
JONATHAN DAVID PUBLISHERS, INC.
Middle Village, New York 11379

Library of Congress Cataloging in Publication Data

Raintree, Diane.
    The household book of hints and tips.

    Bibliography: p.
    Includes index.
    1. Home economics—Handbooks, manuals, etc.
I. Title.
TX158.R34   640'.2   77-29161
ISBN 0-8246-0211-0
Printed in the United States of America

Design By: Arlene Schleifer Goldberg

Contents

- -

Contents

Chapter One

IN
THE
KITCHEN

Part One

Money, Time and Energy Saving Hints

Protecting Glassware

When pouring hot liquids into glassware, cushion the shock caused by the sudden change in

temperature by inserting a spoon (preferably a silver one) into the glass. Pour the hot liquid directly onto the spoon and allow it to flow into the tumbler.

Doubling Recipes

While it is usually safe to double the quantity of ingredients when doubling the yield of a recipe, do not double the amount of salt. A little salt goes a long way, and you will not need twice the amount of salt. Spices should likewise be added sparingly, and not doubled.

Free-flowing Salt

The popular, widely-known method of keeping salt moisture-free and free-flowing is to pour a small amount of uncooked rice into your salt shaker. If you have no rice handy, use aluminum foil to keep moisture out of the salt. Mold a small piece of foil tightly over the top of the shaker and leave it there when the shaker is not in use.

Stuck Tumblers

To loosen glasses that have become stuck together, you will break fewer if you pour cold water into the inner glass and follow this by dipping the bottom of the outer one into hot water. The tumblers come apart without being forced.

1

Transferring Liquids

It is not necessary to make a mess by spilling a liquid when you are transferring it to a narrow-mouthed bottle. Hold a long nail or long pointed pencil alongside the mouth of the container you are pouring from. The liquid will flow down the sides of the nail or pencil in a fine stream and will enter the narrow-mouthed bottle without a drop being spilled.

Small Bottles

Pour the contents of liquids that come in wide-mouthed bottles into bottles with smaller openings. You will waste less when you pour from a bottle with a smaller spout.

Shifty Grinders

A food grinder that will not stay firmly in place is very irritating. You can prevent the problem and keep the grinder from moving around by putting a piece of folded sandpaper, rough side out, between the clamp and the table.

Non-skid Chairs

Chairs, stools and tables need not slide around on kitchen floors, even if the floors are waxed. Rubber tips are available and come in various sizes. These can be attached to the bottom of each leg. Most hardware, drug, and variety stores sell them.

Broom Tips I

Soak a new broom in hot, heavily salted water to give it longer life. In the winter, clean it with a few sweeps in the snow.

Broom Tips II

A rubber tip (like that used on the bottom of crutches) put on a broom handle will prevent the broom from sliding down when propped against the wall.

Broom Tips III

The rough surfaces of sidewalks, driveways, and basements are tough on brooms. To keep brooms from wearing out quickly, dip the ends of the bristles into a shallow pan of thinned shellac, and allow to dry thoroughly.

Spreading Peanut Butter

Avoid wasted energy and save money by adding a teaspoon of hot water to your jar of hardened peanut butter. The peanut butter will spread more easily and will go much further.

Shears and Scissors

Instead of always using a knife to slice, dice, and chop, you may find some kitchen chores are easier to execute with shears. Try it out when

1. cutting raisins and marsh-mallows
2. trimming crusts from bread
3. cutting thin slices of cooked meats and giblets
4. cutting away the pulp and seeds from peppers
5. cutting parsley and chives (nutritionists advise that they lose their flavor when chopped).

If the substance to be cut is sticky, dip the shears in flour first.

Wet Noodles

Wet noodles dropped on a table-cloth or on the floor can be picked up more easily if you sprinkle the area with cornstarch while the noodles are still wet. The corn-starch makes the noodles less slippery and easier to get hold of.

A Stiff Chamois

Soften up a stiff chamois by soaking it in warm water to which a spoonful of olive oil has been added. The chamois will come out soft—and clean.

New Ranges

Some of the new features on ranges can save you money. One feature to inquire about when purchasing a new stove is the device that automatically turns the heat down once the food has begun to cook. These stoves may cost more initially, but they will save you money in the long run.

Stale Sponges

Sponges that are fresh are more pleasant to use, and they do a better job. Freshen-up sponges by soaking them in cold salt water.

Yellow Flame

If the flame on your gas range is yellow, the burner may be clogged. Making sure the gas is turned off, clean the holes through which the gas flows with a pin or a needle. Also, keep the heat-reflector pans under the burners clean. Clean pans will save energy by heating your food faster.

Double Boilers

When using double boilers you can reduce the cooking time by adding salt to the water. Add one level teaspoon of salt for each quart of water.

Heating Water Faster

If you're counting pennies, it's possible to save on fuel costs when heating water. Heat no more water than you will be using at a particular time. You save on fuel because with less water in the pot, the water will heat up faster. Also, remember to cover the pot to reduce evaporation.

3

In the Kitchen

Dishwashing

If you do not have the time to do the dishes as soon as the meal is over, rinse them off and let them soak for a half hour in hot water to which detergent has been added. The work you will have to do later will be greatly reduced. Use hot water for greasy or sugary pans. Use cold water for soaking pans that have had milk, eggs, or flour in them.

Air-dry Dishes

Let dishes air-dry, or dry them with a clean towel. Air-drying is advisable if your kitchen is free of dust, flies, and pets. While the dishes dry, cover them with a clean dry towel.

Pilot Lights

The supply of heat produced by your pilot light can be put to good use. Here are two suggestions:
1. Keep a kettle of water on it, and you will enjoy a continual supply of warm water.
2. Prunes and similar foods, placed in a pot with a small amount of water, will cook slowly for you.

Reduce Cooking Time

To save money and time when broiling, remove from the refrigerator food to be cooked or broiled an hour or two before you plan to put it in the oven. You should be allowing sufficient time for it to warm up and approach room temperature. Your cooking will get done much sooner that way.

Watch Pot Sizes

Cook in flat-bottomed pots, and be sure pans correspond to the size of the burners. Small pots used on large burners waste heat, as do large pots on small burners. Match the pot to the burner as closely as possible.

Reduce Cooking Costs

Whether the stove is gas or electric, the oven retains plenty of heat after you turn it off—provided the oven door is kept *closed*. Make use of that heat to finish the baking by turning the oven off ten minutes before the cooking time is up.

Strengthening Glassware

Glassware can be strengthened so that it will be less fragile and will last longer. Put the glassware in slightly salted water and bring the water to a slow boil. The slower you boil the water the stronger the glassware will be.

Cleaning a Can Opener

Electric can openers get sticky and clogged after repeated use. If you want to avoid the trouble of removing yours from the wall when it needs a cleaning, dip a hard-bristled toothbrush in hot water containing a detergent, and scrub the can opener until clean. However, now and then, it is best to remove the opener from the wall, and to soak it in hot water containing detergent. Allow it to sit for about 10 minutes, and then give it a good scrubbing.

Stubborn Cans

If after you have removed the lid of a can with a can opener you find it difficult to get the food product out (as when opening cans of cranberry jelly and dogfood), turn the can upside down and pierce the bottom of the can. The food will now · loosen and slide out easily after shaking it a few times.

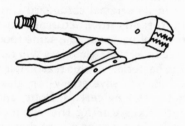

Kitchen Pliers

Locking pliers are handy to have in the kitchen. They are especially useful in loosening the lids of hard-to-open jars. After they are adjusted to the size desired, the jar cover is held in a vise-like grip, and turning it becomes an easy matter. Although locking pliers are usually expensive they are worth having, although ordinary pliers will often do the job well if the jar lid is not too large.

A word of CAUTION: Be very, *very* careful when using pliers on glass jars.

Kitchen Tools

A screwdriver kept in the kitchen is handy for prying off the tops of cans, tightening loose knobs, and tightening loose screws on door hinges. Pliers should also be kept handy to open bottle caps and the like.

Lid Coasters

The plastic lids which come on containers of coffee, peanuts, and shortening cans make good coasters for glasses and cups.

Stubborn Jar Lids

When you are having difficulty getting a good grip on a jar lid, a piece of sandpaper may help. Hold the sandpaper in the palm of your hand and press against the sides of the stubborn lid. It should turn without slipping. If it doesn't work try one of the other tips offered in this section.

Hot Water on Lids

Hard-to-open jar lids are often easily loosened after you have allowed hot water to run on the side of the cap for a minute or two. The sugar or liquid that binds the lid often breaks down under the heat and loosens its grip. If this doesn't work, try one of the other tips in this section.

Prying Jar Lids

A rather successful way of handling hard-to-open jars is to place the flat end of a spoon under the cap and pry it up gently, allowing air to escape. When you hear the hiss of rushing air, you can be sure the lid will yield to your pressure as you turn the cap.

Sticking Corks

Corks in bottles that contain sugary liquids often stick. Put waxed paper around the cork before putting in the cork and the cork will always come off easily.

Enlarging Corks I

Corks shrink with repeated use. To return a cork to its original shape, boil it in a covered pan. This will blow it up and sterilize it at the same time.

Enlarging Corks II

If the cork is too small for the bottle, make it bigger by wrapping as much aluminum foil around the cork as is needed to give it a snug fit.

Lost Corks

To remove a cork that has fallen into a bottle, pour off the liquid. Then, pour in enough ammonia so the cork will float. Let it float for several days. The ammonia will then have reduced the size of the cork and you should be able to retrieve the cork.

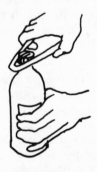

Removing Bottle Caps

Nutcrackers have more than one use—if they're the squeeze type. Use them for turning tight-fitting caps on small-mouthed cans and jars. Avoid squeezing too hard, so as not to dent the metal cap. Of course, if you have a pair of pliers handy, they can be used effectively.

Non-slip Bases

Rest your whipping bowl on a damp, folded cloth to keep it from slipping around while you work. You might also want to tack or staple a large piece of sandpaper to a block of wood of the same size, and keep it handy for kitchen activity.

Airtight Containers

In warm weather, a food product kept in its original cardboard container tends to encourage the growth of bacteria. The same food stored in airtight glass jars will not invite bacteria. For this reason it is a good idea to save screw-top glass jars for storing cereals, flour, and flour mixes during the warmer months. In locations where there is prolonged heat, and where items are not used too often, it is best to refrigerate.

See-through Containers

Try to use glass or see-through containers for dry ingredients. They are more attractive and more practical. You can see what is in the container at a glance, and you can see at a glance when your supply is running low.

Renewing Aluminum

If you have tarnished aluminum trays or foil that you want to bring back to a clean, bright state, boil apple parings in them (or with them) in a large pot of water.

Aluminum Foil Fires

Meats broiled on a sheet of aluminum foil may produce enough melted fat to start a small fire. So, be cautious. First of all, trim all excess fat from the meat before you begin broiling. Secondly, make sure the foil placed beneath the meat has slits cut into it through which the melted fat can drain into the broiler pan.

Save Aluminum Foil

Aluminum foil can be washed off and used again and again. When the foil is no longer suitable for baking, for covering leftovers, or for wrapping food for the freezer, crumple it and use it as a pot scrubber.

A Foil Funnel

If you need a funnel in a hurry and one is not handy, make one out of aluminum foil. Double the foil for added strength, and then roll into a cone, reducing the small end to the required size. You will find it useful for pouring products like salt and sugar from one container into another.

Warped Pans

Allow pots and pans to cool naturally before washing to prevent warping. Pans made of thin metal, such as cake pans, and especially lightweight aluminum containers are prone to bend and go out of shape if not treated correctly.

Preparing Enamelware

Enamelware should be treated before using for the first time. Immerse the product in warm water and bring the water to a slow boil. Preparing your enamelware in this manner will add years to its usefulness.

Seasoning Skillets

If you want new skillets and frying pans (especially those made of cast-iron) to do an effective job, grease them well and place them in your oven for 30 minutes at 450 degrees Fahrenheit. Let them cook, scour them with fine steel wool, and then wash them in warm soapy water.

Cooling Food Naturally

Because oxygen destroys some of the nutrients in food, try not to stir cooked or hot food in order to cool it off. If food is too hot to eat, wait before serving it and allow it to cool naturally.

Homemade Olive Oil

It may not taste exactly like *pure* olive oil, but you may like the taste even better. For one week, soak four large, unstuffed olives in a jar of vegetable oil. Keep the jar tightly covered and refrigerated throughout the entire period—then taste.

Heat Guide

How hot is hot? What is moderate? What is slow cooking? For oven temperatures, here is a chart that may be helpful:

Very Hot . 475 degrees and over
Hot . . . . 400-450 degrees
Moderate 350-375
Slow . . . . 300-325 degrees
Very Slow . . . . 250-275 degrees.

All temperatures are Fahrenheit.

Advance Planning

If you are a busy housekeeper, and you are planning a sit-down meal for guests the next day, you can save energy by setting the table the night before. Turn cups and tumblers and plates over so that dust will not collect in them. Also, cover the silverware with each napkin to keep the utensils dust-free.

Preserving China

China that has been stored in a cool cupboard should be allowed to warm up at room temperature before you pour hot liquids into it.

China Test

When buying chinaware, if the article being sold is advertised as genuine china, you can test it by holding it up to the light. You will see light through it if it is genuine, because genuine china is translucent. In the case of earthenware or imitation china, on the other hand, light will not shine through.

Improving China

Do not be afraid to "spoil" your good china by using it often. Genuine china is strong and does not suffer from regular normal use. Many, in fact, believe that china improves in strength and appearance with usage.

Washing China

Good china is sturdy enough to withstand mild washing as long as the detergent isn't harsh. Rinse with water as hot as your hands can bear. Most pieces of china *can* be washed in the dishwasher, although dishes with decorations may not be able to withstand the hot water that is required.

China Cracks

Hairline cracks in china can often be concealed by boiling the dish in sweet milk. The boiling should last for about an hour at low heat.

Money-saving Coupons

Always check the price of a coupon item against the price of the house brand, because often national brands are more expensive, even with a coupon. If a newspaper has coupons for items you use frequently, get several copies of the paper—that is, if the newspaper is not too costly. All coupons have expiration dates so use them promptly, even if you have to buy more items than you need immediately. You can always stock the extra items in your freezer or pantry or cellar.

Buy Big and Save

You save money when you buy detergents, lotions, etc. in large, economy boxes and bottles. However, it is often awkward to use the product in such large containers. To take advantage of the savings, save small bottles and containers and transfer the contents of the large containers to the small ones.

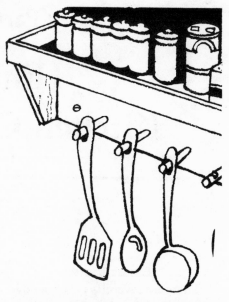

Kitchen Space-savers

Bulky wooden spoons and spatulas that usually congest kitchen drawers can be hung from a rack. A piece of wood cut to the desired width and length will provide a good base for the pegs. Using a ¼-inch drill, make holes in the board every three inches, starting three inches from the end. Hold the drill at a slight downward angle. Then cut off three-inch lengths of ¼-inch dowels and force them into the holes, using a hammer if necessary. Sand the ends of the dowels off if the fit is too tight. Stain or paint the piece, then attach it to your kitchen wall or under a window.

Part Two

Hints on Kitchen Cleanliness

Grease Spots

There are several ways of removing grease. A bit of vinegar added to some water is effective in removing simple grease marks. Jars and bottles that are soiled by grease can be cleaned by adding a spoonful of ammonia to a glass of tap water.

Spattering Grease

Cover the skillet with a colander to keep the grease from spattering when you fry fish or meat. The openings in the colander will allow the steam to escape and permit the food to brown.

Stains on China

Use salt and baking soda to remove stains from china. This is less abrasive than the usual kitchen cleansers.

Washing Glasses

When washing glassware, be sure not to do it together with your greasy dishes. But if you must, do the glasses first so the grease from the dishes will not be transferred to them.

Glassware Luster

You can add sparkle and life to your glassware by rinsing it in water to which a splash of vinegar has been added. Another procedure for adding luster is to put a few pinches of borax in the wash water.

Freshening Containers

To freshen-up bottles and jars, add a little dry mustard to water and permit the solution to stand in the bottles or jars for a few hours.

Cleaning Silverware

Cleaning silver need not be a time-consuming chore. If it's silverware you want to clean, fill an *aluminum* pan with warm water and laundry detergent. The pan should be large enough to hold all the silverware you wish to clean. If the object you wish to clean is very large use a plastic pail and drop in a piece of aluminum foil. After 15 minutes remove the silver pieces from the solution and give them a good rinsing. Your silver will shine.

Another procedure that has been found helpful in cleaning spoons, forks and knives is to place a teaspoon of baking soda and a tablespoon of table salt in a gallon of hot water. Immerse the silverware for 10-15 minutes, rinse and dry thoroughly.

If your silverware has been tarnished by eggs, you will find rubbing them with damp salt an effective way of removing the tarnish.

Cleaning Glassware

To remove brown stains from glassware, rub with dry baking soda. Then, if necessary, follow through with a mild scouring powder, and complete procedure with a thorough rinse. Do not use abrasive pot scrubbers because they will scratch the surface of the glass. Fine steel wool, used carefully, can help greatly.

Cutting-board Stains

To remove stains from cutting-boards, first bleach the stains with a mixture of lemon juice and salt. Rub vigorously into the board and rinse with clean water. If another application is needed, wait until the board has dried.

Prevent Rust Rings

Save the plastic lids that you find on peanut cans, coffee cans, and the like, because they are very useful items. One place where they can be used to great advantage is under cans of scouring powder. The plastic will keep dampness away and will prevent the metal bottom from rusting and leaving an unsightly ring.

aluminum foil

Catch the Spill

If there's a chance a pie or casserole baked in the oven will run over, plan ahead to catch the spill. Place a sheet of aluminum foil, slightly larger than the baking dish, on the shelf *below* the one on which the pie or casserole will be baking. Your stove will stay clean and any spill-over can be removed at once.

Slimy Sponges

Refurbish slimy sponges by soaking them overnight in a mixture of one part vinegar to two parts water. Rinse thoroughly in hot water in the morning.

Protecting Glassware

It's not a good idea to put glassware into hot water bottom first, since that is why glass cracks most often. Glassware can survive the hottest water if you remember to slip it into the water sideways—and slowly.

Glass Teakettles

To remove tea stains from teakettles, fill the pot halfway with water and drop in several pieces of lemon. Boil the water, pour it off, let it cool, then rinse. Rub lemon rind directly on any mineral stains that remain.

Protecting Painted Shelves

Heavy metal cans that are moved around mark up painted shelves. Plastic lids taken from cans of peanuts or coffee or shortening, will protect your shelves if placed under the heavy vegetable and fruit cans on your pantry shelves.

Eliminating Cooking Odors

One of these two ideas may help you get rid of cooking odors without having to install a fan:

1. Boil three teaspoons of ground clove for 15 minutes in two cups of water. This will sweeten the air.
2. If you do not have cloves handy, you might want to try heating vinegar in a pot for five minutes, allowing the vapors to permeate the room.

Keeping Refrigerators Fresh I

Add a teaspoon of baking soda to the soapy wash-water for a thorough deodorizing of your refrigerator. You can cut down on the frequency with which you will have to do this chore by storing food in *closed* containers as much as possible, and by keeping an open box of baking soda on one of the shelves. Baking soda absorbs odors. One box will last for about two months.

Keeping Refrigerators Fresh II

Aside from the baking soda method of keeping odors out of refrigerators, another method is to soak a ball of cotton in vanilla extract, and then place it in a small saucer on a shelf. It will keep the interior smelling sweet.

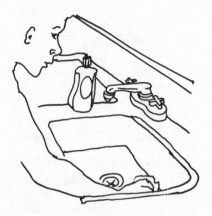

Cleaning Kitchen Sinks

After washing dishes, clean the sink with detergent and warm water. Rinse well. Most marks can be removed by rubbing spots with fine scouring powder on a damp cloth. Coarse scouring materials should be avoided, as they may scratch the finish of porcelain and stainless steel sinks.

Older Sinks

If the sink in your kitchen is old and badly scratched, you will need to use a heavy-duty scouring powder. To make the whole sink whiter, use a standard bleach solution. Fill the sink with hot water, add bleach, and allow it to stand for 10 minutes or more. Drain, then rinse the sink with fresh water.

Kitchen Cabinets

The moisture that usually saturates the atmosphere of a kitchen will take its toll of wooden cabinets whose surfaces are not protected by paint, varnish, shellac or wax. What is often most neglected is the inside of kitchen cabinets which will deteriorate in time when attacked by dry rot and fungus growths. It is worth the trouble of applying shellac to these surfaces which are often left unfinished.

Linoleum Shelves

You can keep your kitchen shelves cleaner and cut down on noise if your counter-tops and shelves are covered with linoleum or tile. The sound will be muffled and the surfaces will wipe clean with ease.

Shining Faucets

To clean faucets effectively, wash down with detergent and rinse with water. Do *not* use scouring powder which may wear off the chrome-plated finish. Remove brown stains around the faucets with a mixture of vinegar (or lemon juice) and water. Rinse with clear water.

In the Kitchen

Avoiding Clogged Drains

Never pour grease or cooking oil down the drain. It will harden and cause clogging. Instead, collect the grease in an empty tin can, allow it to harden, and discard.

Clearing Drain Pipes I

If the kitchen drain becomes clogged, position the water faucet directly over it and run hot water into the drain. If the water drains

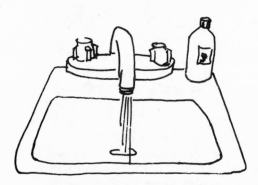

out too slowly, pour hot, sudsy water through the drain. This cuts the grease. Flush well with hot, clean water.

More stubborn clogs may require a special drain cleaner. Try Drano or a similar product. Your hardware dealer will be able to suggest a number of effective products.

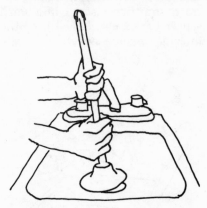

Clearing Drain Pipes II

If your sink gets clogged often, use a rubber plunger. Fit it tightly over the drain hole and force the plunger handle up and down quickly several times. This may loosen clogging. If this does not work, try a snake.

Simple Oven Spills

Let the range cool before you clean it. Wash with warm water and detergent, rinse, and dry with a soft cloth. When wiping off spills from a warm oven, use a dry cloth or paper towel. Remove stubborn spots by rubbing with dry baking soda and a damp cloth.

Cleaning Gas Ranges

Remove the grates and burner bowls on a gas range and wash in warm, sudsy water. If they are hard to clean, allow to soak 30 minutes in a mixture of one cup vinegar and one gallon hot water.

Fig. 1

Cleaning Stained Woodwork

The woodwork in kitchens is often stained by grease and dirtied by smoke. Rectify this by spreading a solution of starch and water on the woodwork and letting it dry. Then, rub with a soft brush or cloth. The stain will usually come off with the starch.

Burners may be cleaned in the same way. If the holes in the burner heads are stopped up, clean them with a fine wire, toothpick, a pin, or a needle (see Fig. 1). After cleaning, rinse the burners in hot water. Put them in a warm oven, 300 degrees Fahrenheit, and allow to dry for 15 minutes. It is important for water in the burner to be completely dried out so that it will operate properly when replaced.

Eliminating Room Odors

A dish of vinegar left standing in a room will dispel the odor of smoke. To get the smoke out of a room quickly, soak a towel in water, wring it out, then swish it around the room.

Odors on Hands

There are several ways to remove the odors of onions and fish from your hands. First, you can try to simply rinse your hands well and then wash with soap. If that doesn't work, try rinsing your hands with vinegar. And if *that* doesn't work, try rubbing your palms with damp salt.

Fruit Stains

Fruit stains can be removed from your hands by rubbing on a mixture of lemon juice and salt, then rinsing off with water.

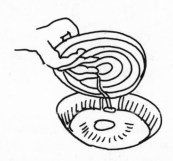

Heating Units on Electric Ranges

Some heating units tilt up and others pull out (see illustration). Make sure the range is turned off and the unit is cool before you remove it. Clean with a damp cloth. Heating elements should never be submerged in water.

Wooden Handles

Because the metal part of a knife is attached to the wooden handle with an adhesive, it is not a good idea to soak it in water for a prolonged period. Water may weaken the adhesive. Painted knife handles are also likely to be damaged by protracted soaking.

Cleaning the Oven

Ovens require a thorough cleaning from time to time to remove

accumulated grease and burned-on food. Place ½ cup household ammonia in a bowl and set the bowl in a cold oven. Allow to stand at least four hours, or overnight. Remove the bowl and add one quart warm water to the contents. Use this solution to clean the inside walls of the oven. Scouring powder or steel wool may be used to remove stubborn stains.

Stains on Formica

Instant drinks and gelatin desserts leave stains on formica counter-tops. If an abrasive cleanser rubbed with a wet rag doesn't remove the stain, buy a laminate plastic cleaner with tylol-exyol base. Your paint store dealer will be able to suggest a product with this basic ingredient. Apply it with a clean rag, rub, and the stain should come off.

Lining Crumb Trays

Crumb trays on your stove top collect more than crumbs. When foods on your stove boil over, that's where the spill will go. To keep from having to scrub messy crumb trays, line them with aluminum foil.

Shelf Paper

For dishes stored on shelves to stay clean, it is important to line your shelves. When shelf-paper tends to curl up, secure it with cellophane tape, rather than thumb tacks. When dishes are shifted around, the paper will not tear as easily if tape is used.

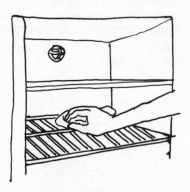

Cleaning the Refrigerator

Use a mixture of two tablespoons of baking soda and one quart of warm water to clean the inside surface of the refrigerator. Rub hard-to-clean spots with dry soda. Rinse, then dry with a soft cloth.

Shelves, drawers, and other parts of the refrigerator should be removed and can be washed with the same solution or with a milder detergent.

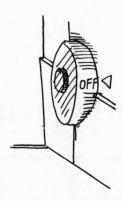

To keep frozen food from thawing, wrap in layers of newspaper and place in a cardboard box, and pack them close together.

Place a pan under the freezing section to catch melting ice, then place a large pan of hot water in the freezer. Allow to thaw. Do not scrape or punch the ice with a knife or sharp tool, as this may damage the freezing unit.

Defrosting the Refrigerator

When you are planning to defrost, make sure the control dial is turned to Off, or Defrost. Remove all ice cube trays and frozen food.

Beaters and Choppers

Immerse egg beaters, potato mashers, grinders, food choppers, etc., in cold water as soon as you are through using them. Clean difficult-to-get-at spots with a toothbrush. The same applies to food choppers and grinders.

Part Three

Hints on Refrigerating and Freezing

━━━━━━━━━━━━━━━━━━━━━━━━━━━━━━━

Freezer Space

One cubic foot of freezer space will hold 35-40 pounds of meat or 40 pint cartons of various foods.

Avoid Soft Packages

Buy only packages that are frozen solid. Avoid packages that feel soft, indicating they have started to thaw. Refreezing after thawing lowers quality and saps the taste.

Avoid Stained Packages

Do not buy packages of frozen foods that are stained. The stains are an indication that the package had once defrosted, to some degree, and was then refrozen.

Freezer Temperature

A storage temperature of lower than 0 degrees Fahrenheit is needed to maintain the best quality in frozen foods. Freezer temperatures of 0 degrees Fahrenheit or

above do not kill the bacteria in food, but simply stop their multiplication.

Unfavorable changes in eating quality take place more rapidly in food stored at temperatures above 0 degrees Fahrenheit. Slow growth of microorganisms may occur at temperatures above 10 degrees Fahrenheit, causing foods to lose color, flavor, characteristic texture, and nutritive value.

Temperature Check

Find out if the storage space you have for frozen foods provides the recommended temperature—or, if not, how close it comes to it. You'll need to know this temperature to help determine how long you may store the foods.

To check, use an accurate thermometer and take the temperature in several locations. Regulate the temperature control to maintain the warmest spot of 0 degrees Fahrenheit, if possible.

Storage Time

How long commercially frozen food will retain good quality in the home at 0 degrees Fahrenheit or lower depends on the kind of food it is, and how long and at what temperature it was stored before you bought it.

The table on the next page suggests maximum home storage periods for frozen foods that are of good quality when purchased. They are for foods that have been subject to good commercial freezing, handling, and storage before you purchased them. If there is any question about the quality of the frozen food, keep it in your freezer for less time than indicated.

If your equipment does not maintain a temperature of 0 degrees Fahrenheit or lower, plan to hold frozen foods only a few days before you use them.

Suggested Maximum Home-Storage Periods To Maintain Good Quality in Purchased Frozen Foods

Food	Approximate holding period at 0° F.	Food	Approximate holding period at 0° F.
Baked goods		**Poultry**	
Bread and yeast rolls:		Chicken:	
White bread	3	Cut-up	9
Cinnamon rolls	2	Livers	3
Plain rolls	3	Whole	12
Cakes:		Duck, whole	6
Angel	2	Goose, whole	6
Chiffon	2	Turkey:	
Chocolate layer	4	Cut-up	6
Fruit	12	Whole	12
Pound	6	Cooked chicken and turkey:	
Yellow	6	Chicken or turkey dinners	
Danish pastry	3	(sliced meat and gravy)	6
Doughnuts:		Chicken or turkey pies	6
Cake type	3	Fried chicken	4
Yeast raised	3	Fried chicken dinners	4
Pies (unbaked):			
Apple	8	**Fish**	
Boysenberry	8	Fish:	
Cherry	8	Fillets:	
Peach	8	Cod, flounder, haddock, halibut, pollack	6
Meat		Mullet, ocean perch, sea trout, striped bass	3
Beef:		Pacific Ocean perch	2
Hamburger or chipped (thin) steaks	4	Salmon steaks	2
Roasts	12	Sea trout, dressed	3
Steaks	12	Striped bass, dressed	3
Lamb:		Whiting, drawn	4
Patties (ground meat)	4		
Roasts	9		

Power Failure

Should the electricity fail in your house, and your refrigerator and freezer are not operating, avoid opening the doors as much as possible. Your food will last much longer if you can retain the cold.

Freezing Procedure

Freeze only high-quality fresh meat and fish. Freezing does *not* improve quality.

Keep all food to be frozen—and anything that touches it—clean. Freezing does *not* sterilize food; the extreme cold simply slows down all action that would normally affect the quality of the food or cause it to spoil.

Wrapping for Freezing

Wrap meat and fish to be frozen in moisture-vapor-resistant coverings to make the package air-tight and prevent drying. Place two layers of waxed paper between individual chops, steaks, and fillets so that individual frozen pieces can be separated easily, then wrap in freezer paper.

Fast Freezing

For foods to freeze more quickly, arrange to have the containers touch the sides of the freezer, and keep food towards the back, if possible.

Cool off cooked foods as quickly as possible after cooking, and freeze at once.

Freezer Cellophane

Foods to be frozen can be wrapped in cellophane provided you select the type of cellophane that has been designed specifically for freezer use. Read the package label before making your cellophane purchase.

Plastic Wrap and Plastic Bags

Plastic wrap (like Saran or Handi-wrap) is so sturdy you do not need to use an overwrapper with it to package the foods you are planning to freeze.

Freezer Foil

A special aluminum foil is made specifically for wrapping foods to be frozen. It is extra heavy for freezer durability. You can find it in most supermarkets.

Charcoal in Freezers

One or two pieces of charcoal placed in your freezer will absorb any unpleasant odors and keep the interior smelling sweet and fresh.

Freezer Economy

For economy, use freezer to capacity. A well-filled freezer oper-

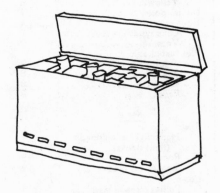

ates more efficiently than one that is partly filled.

Sealing Tape

In sealing packages to be frozen, make sure you are using a tape specifically designed for freezing. If you use the wrong type, it will become unstuck at low temperatures.

Glass Jars

Glass freezer jars have wider mouths than regular canning jars. The advantage is that the contents of such containers can be removed even before they are fully thawed.

Freezing Liquids

Clean, empty coffee cans are handy, useful containers in which liquids can be frozen. You must be sure that you do not neglect to secure the edges with sealing tape.

Freezer Organization

Create specific sections in the freezer for different foods. You will save much time, because you will know just where to look for meats, breads, desserts, etc. Also, try to keep the foods that have been stored the longest closer to the top and front of the freezer.

Freezing Small Units

It is to your advantage to prepare food to be frozen in small packages. These will freeze and thaw more quickly than foods frozen in large containers or packages.

Meat Leftovers

Cooked leftovers of meat (and poultry) can be stored frozen for several weeks in a covered container. They can also be wrapped in aluminum foil and stored in a freezer bag.

Labeling Frozen Foods

To keep your freezer orderly, take the trouble to mark on each package of frozen food what the package contains and the date on

which it was frozen. And, if you have the patience, keep a running inventory of the food inside the freezer, the date put in, and the date removed.

Poultry Pieces

To freeze, place meaty pieces, such as the breast, legs, and wings, close together in a freezer bag or freezer wrap. To shorten thawing time, place double layer of freezer wrap or waxed paper between the pieces so they can be easily separated for thawing. Seal, label, and freeze.

Boned Poultry

Poultry takes up less freezer space if the bones are removed. It keeps best if it is removed from the bones and packed solidly to eliminate as much air as possible. Contact with air causes a rancid off-flavor to develop. Addition of broth or gravy lengthens storage life by preventing contact with air.

Selecting Poultry

Freeze only fresh, high-quality poultry. Use well-fleshed birds with few skin blemishes.

Choose poultry according to how you plan to use the frozen product. Young chickens or turkeys are suitable for roasting, frying, and broiling. Mature poultry can be used for braising and stewing.

Poultry that is correctly frozen and is stored only for the recommended time can be as good as fresh poultry.

Refreezing

Frozen raw or cooked poultry that has thawed may be safely refrozen if it still contains the crystals or if it is still below 40 degrees Fahrenheit—and has been held no longer than one or two days at refrigerator temperatures after thawing. Thawing and refreezing may lower the eating quality of the food.

New Recipes

When you try a new recipe of a food you are planning to freeze, and you are not sure whether it will freeze well or not, keep a record of the method you used. If the recipe worked, you will be able to follow the same steps when you want to try it again.

Freezing Small Cuts of Meat

Small cuts of meat that are to be kept for more than three days should be frozen. Meats stored frozen only a week or two can be wrapped in heavy waxed paper first, then wrapped again with aluminum foil. Wrap chops and patties separately with inner wrapping paper, then overwrap several at a time with foil. Use special freezer wrapping paper for long-term storage.

Frozen TV Dinners

Individual, complete meals can be stored in a freezer. These will be especially useful when unexpected guests show up at meal time, or when members of the family must take their own meals.

Thawing Meats and Fish

Most frozen meats and fish may be cooked either with or without previous thawing. But extra cooking time must be allowed for meats not thawed first—just how much will depend on the size and shape of the cut.

Large frozen roasts may take as much as 1 ½ times as long to cook as unfrozen cuts of the same weight and shape. Small roasts and thin cuts, such as steaks and chops, require less time.

Frozen fish, fillets, and steaks may be cooked as if they were in the unfrozen form if additional cooking time is allowed. When fish are to be breaded and fried, or stuffed, it is more convenient to thaw them first to make handling easier.

It is best to thaw frozen meats and fish in the refrigerator in their original wrappings.

For most satisfactory results, cook thawed meat and fish immediately.

Cutting Knives

There are knives specifically designed for cutting frozen foods. After cutting off the portion of the frozen package you will be using, remember to cover with freezer paper the exposed end of the frozen food that you will be returning to the freezer.

Long-term Freezing

Frozen meat wrapped in moisture-proof freezer paper can be stored for fairly long periods, if kept in a home freezer set at 0 degrees Fahrenheit or lower. Don't store frozen meats for long periods in the freezer compartment of a refrigerator.

Freezing Soups

Your ice-cube trays make handy containers for freezing soups. Make sure to cover trays. Individual servings can be removed in the form of cubes, one or more at a time, while the rest are kept frozen for future servings.

Freezing Fried Foods

Although it is not unsafe, it is best not to freeze fried foods. They sometimes turn rancid when frozen even for very short periods and require careful watching.

Freezing Meat Patties

Meat patties and similar uncooked foods should be stacked in layers with two thicknesses of wrapping separating the layers. This will enable you to separate them easily after they are frozen.

Broiling Frozen Steaks

There is no need to thaw frozen steaks or chops before broiling them. Simply allow them longer cooking time.

Cherries and Berries

Wash cherries and berries in ice-cold water before freezing them. You'll waste fewer that way because the freezing process will then take less time.

Freezing Fruit Pies

Fruit pies will be easier to handle if you place them in the freezer for a short time until frozen, then remove and wrap with freezer paper. They will not crumble if you follow this procedure.

Freezing Baked Goods

Leftovers of your homemade baked goods, such as wedges of pie, turnovers, bar-type cookies, or thin cookies can be frozen individually.

Store-bought baked goods, coffee cakes, sliced bread, rolls and the like, can be stored for short periods in the sealed cardboard containers in which you purchased them.

When Freezing Cheese

To maintain its proper consistency, cheese should be frozen as quickly as possible. Large pieces of cheese should therefore be cut into ½-pound chucks which are no thicker than one inch, to hasten the freezing process.

Be sure to wrap the cheese *tightly* in a moistureproof material such as foil or plastic wrap, and then cover it in freezer paper. This will prevent the cheese from losing moisture, and will insure freshness.

Which Cheese to Freeze

Most firm or semi-firm cheeses can be kept frozen for as long as six to eight weeks, provided they are properly wrapped. Soft to semi-soft cheeses, and blue-veined cheeses, are generally more fragile, and may or may not take well to

freezing. It is better to first freeze them in small quantities and then test for flavor and consistency, before freezing a large supply.

Freezing Corn Kernels

Corn loses its flavor quickly once it is picked, and should therefore be frozen as soon as possible after harvest. Freeze only ears which are mature. The kernels should be fully-developed, and their "milk" should be thin and sweet. Blanch by boiling in hot water for four minutes, plunge into ice water, and then freeze.

Freezing Corn on the Cob

After removing the husk, wrap each ear separately in freezer foil. Put the wrapped ears in water at a fast boil and blanch for eight minutes. Then chill the wrapped ears in ice water before freezing.

Thawing Corn on the Cob

Put the frozen ears directly from the freezer into cold water and bring the water to its boiling point. The corn will thaw as the water heats up.

Freezing Coffee Beans

If you grind your own coffee and purchase the beans in quantity, you can freeze the unground beans. In fact, coffee beans keep better frozen than on the cabinet shelf.

Vegetables Not to Freeze

Several vegetables that are eaten raw don't take well to freezing. These include lettuce, celery, cucumbers and carrots. They lose their crispness when frozen. The same is true of a tomato (which is a fruit). If they are to be cooked, it will not matter.

Cooking Frozen Vegetables

Don't thaw out frozen vegetables before cooking, except for corn on the cob and spinach. Cook in as little water as possible for as short a time as is necessary to bring the vegetables to the tender but crunchy point.

Portable "Freezer"

Empty milk cartons filled with water and frozen make handy portable "freezers" to take on picnics for keeping beverages cool.

Vegetable Stew for Freezing.

Don't cook the vegetables completely if you are going to freeze the stew. When the stew is thawed and reheated, they'll finish cooking at that time. Don't put potatoes in the frozen stew. Add fresh-cooked potatoes when the stew is reheated.

Ice Savers for Hot Days

Fill a plastic gallon jug (such as milk comes in) with water, and freeze. When frozen, move it from the freezer to your refrigerator. As the ice melts in the container, you'll have a good supply of cold drinking water that you can pour off as needed.

As you use the water in the jug, continue to refill it with fresh water until the ice is completely melted. This generally takes three or four days. Keep another jug in the freezer while the first one is defrosting.

Ice Savers for Parties

If you will be needing ice cubes for a large party you are planning, unload your ice tray each time the cubes are formed, and store them in

plastic bags in the freezing compartment of your refrigerator. They will last for a long time.

Refrigerator Efficiency

For maximum cooling power with a minimum of electric power, the cold air must be able to circulate freely in a refrigerator. It is therefore wise to keep items stored *uncrowded* on the shelves.

Before Refrigerating

Save on power by cooling off foods before you put them in the refrigerator. Refrigerators use more energy when they have to cool hot foods. And unless your refrigerator defrosts automatically, when you put hot foods into your appliance, you will have to do your own defrosting much more often.

Self-Defrost Refrigerators and Freezers

Self-defrost refrigerators and freezers are more costly to operate than regular models. Much more electricity is required to operate the self-defrost units. Bear this in mind when buying your next unit. If you feel that owning a self-defrost model would be a greater time-saver, investigate one of the energy-efficient models now on the market.

Airtight Refrigerators

Refrigerators are fitted with a rubber gasket to make a tight seal when the door is closed. But gas-

gasket

kets become worn, and when this happens some of the cold will escape. This means more power has to be used to keep the refrigerator temperature low. It is, therefore, wise to check your refrigerator door from time to time. Shut the refrigerator door on a piece of paper. If you can pull the paper out when the door is shut, the door needs a new gasket.

Locating a Refrigerator

The best spot to place a refrigerator in your kitchen is not near the stove, and not near any other heating appliance. Locate the refrigerator near the coolest kitchen wall where space is available.

Storing Vegetable Oils

All vegetable oils should be kept in the refrigerator, especially in warm climates. Unrefrigerated, it is only a matter of time before oils, including olive oil, become rancid. The cloudiness that you see on oils that have been chilled a bit too much does not affect the oil. Cloudy oil left at room temperature for an hour will turn clear again.

Storing Meat and Fish

It is important for raw meat and fish products to be refrigerated, preferably at 35–40 degrees Fahrenheit. So keep your roasts, chops, and steaks, your poultry, fish, and unsmoked meats in the refrigerator. Pack them loosely because they need air to keep in prime condition. Loosen tight transparent coverings. This applies only to raw food items that will be used within three or four days. If you plan to store these food items for a longer period, it is advisable to freeze them. Cooked food items can be refrigerated for a week or two.

Part Four

Kitchen Tips on Dairy Products

Storing Milk

Take milk out of the refrigerator only when you are ready to use it. Left standing at room temperature, milk quickly loses its freshness. Store it in the coldest part of the refrigerator and *keep it covered,* otherwise it will quickly take on the flavor of other foods.

Boiling Milk

To keep boiled milk from sticking to the sides of the pan, rinse the pan in cold water before pouring in the milk. To prevent milk from boiling over, turn off the heat as soon as the milk starts to boil.

Dry Milk

Keep dry milk in unopened packages at room temperature, preferably not above 75 degrees Fahrenheit. Once you have opened the package, be careful to reseal it tightly, and keep it in a tightly covered can or jar in the refrigerator.

Scalding Milk

The place to scald milk is in the top part of a double boiler. The milk will not boil over, nor will it scorch the pot. Of course, there must be water boiling in the lower part.

Scorched Milk

Burnt taste can be removed from scorched milk by placing the hot pan of milk in cold water and adding a pinch of salt.

Fruit in Fresh Cream

Often when poured over fruits and berries, cream tends to curdle. You can prevent this by adding a pinch of baking soda to the cream first.

Whipping Cream

Use four drops of lemon juice per half pint (one cup) of cream. This will make cream whip more rapidly. Count the drops, because too much lemon juice will sour the cream. If you have an eyedropper, use it to count the drops.

Spreading Butter

In order to soften butter so it will spread more easily, cut the amount you will be using off the bar, and allow it to sit at room temperature for about 10 minutes before using it. Do not allow the *entire* quarter pound section to remain out of the refrigerator, because it will lose its freshness and will become rancid more quickly.

Evaporated Milk

Cover opened cans of evaporated milk before storing them in the refrigerator. Use waxed paper, plastic wrap or aluminum foil and secure it with a rubber band. The covering will stop the milk from drying around the lip where the can was opened, and will prevent the flavors of other foods in the refrigerator from penetrating the milk.

Storing Hard Cheese

Wrap cheese in waxed paper, aluminum foil, or plastic wrap so that air will not get to it. Then, store it in the refrigerator. Packaged cheese can be kept in its original wrapping, but use additional wrapping if the original has been torn or opened once.

Storing Soft Cheeses

Soft cheese should be stored like milk: in a tightly-covered container in the refrigerator. Purchase only as much as you will be using within a few days so as not to run the risk of having the cheese spoil.

Cheeses at Flavor Peak

Cheese tastes best at room temperature. Remove from the refrigerator as much as you plan to use about 15 minutes before you'll be serving it. Cottage cheese is the exception; it is best served chilled.

Cheese and Fruit

Some cheeses taste better with particular fruits than others. You might want to try:
1. Swiss with orange sections
2. Camembert with apples
3. Roquefort with pears
4. Liederkranz with grapes

Serve apples, pears, and cheese cut into pieces and speared on toothpicks.

Toxicity in Cheese-mold

Until recently, it was considered safe to cut away that part of a cheese that had become moldy, and to consume the rest. Recent studies by the FDA, however, show that certain types of cheese-mold produce toxic substances which may be harmful to humans. It would, therefore, be wise to discard moldy cheese altogether, rather than risk one's health.

Cheese Recipe Guide

When purchasing a hard cheese for a recipe that calls for shredded cheese, remember that four ounces or ¼ pound of hard cheese will yield one cup when shredded.

Use the following as a guide for purchasing cottage or cream cheese:

1 pound cottage cheese = 2 cups

3 ounces cream cheese = 6 tablespoons

8 ounces cream cheese = 1 cup or 16 tablespoons.

Dried Out Cheese

Why throw away dried out cheese! Grate it and store it in a covered container for later use in cooking.

Grating Cheese

Chilled cheese will grate more easily. Grate it as soon as you take it out of the refrigerator.

Cooking Dairy Products

When you cook with milk or cheese, keep the heat at a very low temperature. This will prevent the food from curdling or scorching. Don't overcook.

Part Five

Kitchen Tips on Meat

- -

For Best Taste

To derive the best taste from your meat products, cook as soon as you can after making your purchase. Smaller cuts should be used first. Steaks and chops can be refrigerated for only two or three days before cooking or broiling, while roasts will keep a bit longer.

Variety Meats

Liver, kidney, heart, and sweetbreads spoil more rapidly than other meats. They should be prepared and cooked on the day of purchase and stored promptly in the coldest part of the refrigerator.

Ground Meat Varieties

There is much you can do with ground meats other than broil or pan-cook them in patties. Try making meat loaf, Swedish meat balls, hash, chili, stuffed cabbage, and stuffed peppers.

Extracting Meat Flavor

To get all the full flavor out of broiled meats, season with salt *after* broiling, not before.

Signs of Good Beef

You can be reasonably sure of the high quality of beef if:
1. the lean part is light red
2. the lean part looks velvety
3. the lean part is veined with fat
4. the fat is flaky
5. the bones are red.

Storing Cooked Meats

Cooked meat is perishable and must be stored in the refrigerator in a covered container, or should be wrapped tightly in aluminum foil or waxed paper.

Storing Smoked Meats

Smoked meats—such as ham, frankfurters, and bacon—and sausage, smoked or unsmoked—may be kept tightly-wrapped during storage. They keep longer than unsmoked meats. Bacon and sausage, however, are likely to alter in flavor.

Storing Venison

An excellent product to keep in your freezer is venison. It will retain its freshness for almost a whole year and will serve as an unusually attractive main dish all throughout the year.

INSPECTION MARK

Beef Grades

According to the United States Department of Agriculture, the following is a breakdown of beef grading:

U.S. Prime—Excellent quality and usually tender and juicy, good distribution of fat through the lean meat.

U.S. Choice—This grade combines a moderate amount of fat with desirable eating quality. If you find graded beef at your butcher's, it is most likely to be U.S. Choice.

U.S. Good—Cuts preferred by consumers who enjoy relatively tender beef with a high ratio of lean to fat.

U.S. Commercial—Most beef of this grade is produced from mature animals. It has a fairly thick, fat covering and lacks natural tenderness. Such meat is low-priced, and usually requires long, slow cooking.

For Wholesomeness

Meat that has passed federal inspection for wholesomeness is stamped with a round purple mark: "U.S. INSP'D & P'S'D". The round mark is stamped only on carcasses and major cuts, and you may not find it on such cuts as roasts and steaks.

GRADE MARK

Buy With Caution

Some suppliers advertise a "beef bundle" or a "steak package." Unless these ads specify the grade of the meat and the kind and amount of the various cuts included, you would be well advised to buy with caution.

For Quality

Meat can be wholesome even if it is of low quality. Do not be misled by implications that the USDA inspection mark is an assurance of quality. Meat grading is the function of a separate division of the U.S. Department of Agriculture.

The USDA grade mark, which is a guide to the quality of meat—its tenderness, juiciness, and flavor—appears in a shield-shaped design.

Government vs. Private Markings

The United States Department of Agriculture (USDA) grade name appears in purple on most of the retail cuts of meat. All graded meat is inspected, but not all inspected meat is graded. Meat packers, wholesalers, or retailers may use their own brand names and this should not be confused with USDA grades. Letters such as AA and A are never used as meat grades by the USDA.

Meat Prices and Quality

If some cuts of meat cost more than others, the difference is not necessarily in the *quality* of the meat, but in the quantity available at a particular time, and also in the amount available on a particular animal. Loin steaks and center-cut chops cost more because there is less of it on each animal. There are only about 40 pounds of porterhouse, T-bone, and club steaks on a steer that weighs in at 1,000 pounds. A 250-pound porker dresses down to only about 10 pounds of center-cut chops, and a 100-pound lamb yields only about three pounds of loin chops.

Do not fear buying lower priced meats, because it is not an indication of quality.

Beef Roasting Procedure

Sprinkle the meat with salt and pepper before placing it fat side up in an open roasting pan or on an oven rack. Insert the meat thermometer through the outside fat into the thickest part of the meat, being sure the thermometer point does not rest on bone or fat. Roast at 325 degrees Fahrenheit without adding water or covering the pan.

A sirloin tip, standing rib, or rolled rib roast of about six pounds will be rare when the meat thermometer reaches 140 degrees, medium at 160 degrees, and well done at 170.

Veal Roasting Procedure

Regardless of the cut, follow the preparation directions for roasting beef. Your oven should be set at 325 degrees Fahrenheit until the meat thermometer reaches 180 degrees.

Lamb Roasting Procedure

Follow preparation directions for roasting beef. Roast at 325 degrees Fahrenheit. Roasted leg of lamb will be medium done when the meat thermometer reaches 175 degrees, whether the cut is an eight or nine pound full leg or a five or six pound "American" leg.

Roasting Fresh Pork

Follow preparation directions for roasting beef. Keep the oven temperature at 325 degrees Fahrenheit throughout the roasting. Pork loin, as well as shoulder or crown roast cuts of about four pounds, will be done when the meat thermometer reaches 185 degrees. If there is even so much as a tinge of pink to the meat, increase roasting time until the pink color disappears.

Broiling Steaks and Chops

Proper broiling temperature is 550 degrees Fahrenheit. When the meat is on the broiler rack and the rack is in place, there should be about two inches between the surface of the meat and the heat. If the chops or steaks are very thick, decrease the distance.

When broiling in a gas range, keep the door closed. When broiling in an electric range, leave the door slightly ajar. When the meat is well-browned, season it with salt and pepper, then turn and brown the other side. Turn only once. Serve the meat as soon as it's done for maximum succulence.

Seasoning Meat

To enhance the flavor of beef and veal choose from these seasonings—celery, onion, garlic, green pepper, parsley, basil, bay leaves, marjoram, peppercorns, and thyme.

Simmering Meat

Simmered meat is more flavorful and juicy when it is chilled quickly in the stock in which it was cooked, than if stock is drained from meat before chilling.

Tenderized Meat

Meat sometimes is treated before cooking so as to increase tenderness. Some tenderizing treatments are applied by the butcher before the meat is sold; others are applied in the home. In the home, round steak and flank steak can be made more tender by pounding them with a mallet. Steaks can also be scored by cutting slashes across the surface or by pounding the steak with a mallet. Applying these various procedures before braising helps make steaks more tender.

Tenderizing With Vinegar

If you suspect meat may be tough, try rubbing in some vinegar before cooking. Also, marinating the meat in wine vinegar produces an interesting and flavorful taste.

Tenderizing With Lemon

Lemon juice poured over veal cutlet and allowed to stand for 30 minutes will make the meat tender and delicious.

Part Six

Kitchen Tips on Fish

Purchasing Fresh Fish

It is important to recognize the signs of freshness in fish. Here are a few hints that are generally helpful:

1. Eyes should be bright, clear and bulging.
2. Gills should be reddish-pink and not slimy.
3. Scales should be bright and shiny and not loose.
4. Flesh should be firm to the touch. It should spring back when pressed in.

Washing Fish

Fish and seafood are usually clean and need only be dipped in water and wiped dry before cooking. Holding either fish or seafood under running water for extended periods of time detracts from its succulence.

Storing Fresh Fish

Fresh fish should be refrigerated. Place in coldest part of refrigerator and use within two days. Do not freeze if you can avoid it, but if you must, freeze it as soon as possible after purchasing.

For Maximum Flavor

For maximum flavor, eat fresh fish the same day you buy it. The flavor decreases in a few days, although the fish remains fresh.

Freezing Fish

When freezing fish, dip it in water and dry off with absorbent paper or a towel. Then, wrap it in freezer paper.

Thawing Fish

Frozen fish should be thawed only long enough to take away its surface icy hardness. If thawed too long before cooking the flavor will disappear along with the melting ice.

Do not soak the fish in water. Let it defrost in a pan at room temperature and use the collected juices, which are rich in vitamins, to make sauces or soups.

Fish Odor

To keep your hands from smelling fishy, soak the fish in cold water to chill it before you handle it further.

Slippery Fish

You can prevent the fish from slipping through your fingers by dipping your fingers in salt.

Fish Scales

Fish scales will come off easily if you dip the fish in hot water very briefly before beginning to clean it.

Storing Live Shellfish

Keep live shellfish in the refrigerator at a medium temperature, and *not* in water.

Cooking Fish

Fish, unlike meat, does not become more *tender* with cooking. Fish becomes more flavorful as it is cooked, but only to a point. Overcooking it adds nothing to the flavor, and only toughens it.

Fish and Butter

Use plenty of butter when cooking fish and fish sauces. Butter brings out the best in fish of all varieties.

Fillet vs. Whole Fish

Although whole fish is cheaper than fillets or steaks, do not forget that there is considerable waste in whole fish. There is no waste in fillets, and only a small amount of waste in steaks. Keep these facts in mind when comparing prices.

Fish Garnish

Tomatoes, mushroom caps, and baked potatoes, split and topped with cheese can be placed around the broiling fish. This will add greatly to the flavor of your dish.

Baking the Fish Whole

Remove the head of the fish only *after* baking. Removing it beforehand will leave you with dry and toughened fish at the cut end. By leaving the head on, you seal in the flavor and juices, and also reduce the amount of cooking time required.

Pan-fried Fish

Before pan-frying, dip fillets, fish steaks, shellfish, and split or whole small fish in milk, to which has been added a beaten egg and two tablespoons of water. After dipping, roll the fish in bread or cracker crumbs. Fry in hot oil until light brown on both sides, making sure the fat doesn't burn.

Sauteed Fish

Fry the fish in melted butter, but do not put the butter on the fish. Be certain that the fat does not burn. Turn the fish once. Before serving, pour the pan drippings over the fish.

Smoking Fat

The odor that fried fish may give off does not come primarily from the fish, but from the smoking fat. To keep deep fat from reaching the smoking point, keep an eye on the flame. Make sure the heat is not too intense.

Fish Fillets and Shellfish

When broiling fish fillet, remember that generally it does not have to be turned, and neither do broiled shrimp, scallops, split or spiny lobsters. Broil three to ten minutes depending on thickness, until fish flakes easily when pricked with a fork, or until shellfish feels tender when pierced with a fork.

Broiling Fish

Depending on the thickness, broil *thick* fish steaks and whole fish for three to eight minutes before turning. Turn only once. After turning, brush with butter and sprinkle with seasonings.

Baking Fish

Bake fish at 350 degrees Fahrenheit for 10-20 minutes per pound. Bake tiny fish at the same temperature for one or two minutes per ounce. When fish flakes easily, it is done.

Part Seven

Kitchen Tips
on Poultry

Selecting a Chicken

Before buying a whole chicken, check out the thighs and neck. Neither should be thin or scrawny. Also, check the skin color before making a purchase. You'll find that chickens with a light yellow skin-color have the best meat.

Best Poultry Sizes

When purchasing ready-to-cook chicken for broiling, allow ¼ to ½ of a bird per serving. When buying ready-to-cook birds for roasting, stewing, or frying, purchase ¾ of a pound per serving. Small sizes are best for broiling. Young birds have smooth, tender skin, soft tender meat, and a flexible breastbone.

Thawing Frozen Poultry

Frozen poultry should be completely thawed before cooking. Take the bird out of the freezer, leave it in its original wrapping and place it in the refrigerator. A whole chicken will require overnight to thaw out at room temperature, and a day to thaw if kept in the refrigerator. A large turkey will take several days to completely unfreeze if kept in the refrigerator, and much less time at room temperature. But it is always better to permit the fowl to thaw out slowly in the refrigerator.

Foil Baked Chicken

Before baking, brush the chicken halves (or quarters) with melted butter and sprinkle on salt, pepper and seasonings—including garlic, if desired. Wrap the pieces in foil so that the juices will not be lost. Bake for 50 minutes at 400 degrees Fahrenheit in a shallow pan or on a cookie sheet. When baking is finished, pull back the foil and brown the chicken in the broiler. Baste the bird during broiling with its own juices.

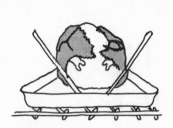

Roasting Ducks and Geese

Place a V-shaped rack in the roasting pan and put the bird breast-up on the rack. Prick the breast skin of a large goose in several places so that the fat can drain off. During roasting, do *not* brush the bird with the melted fat.

During the first half of the roasting period, protect the breast and legs with a loose piece of aluminum foil, then remove it. Prick the skin a second time and finish the roasting at 350 degrees Fahrenheit.

A goose of approximately six or seven pounds requires three hours roasting time, beginning at 325 degrees Fahrenheit.

Begin the roasting of ducks at 325 degrees and allow two hours for a three-pound duck, and three hours for a bird that weighs over four pounds.

Baked Chicken

First, brown pieces to be baked in a skillet, then put the whole bird or pieces in an open or covered casserole for oven baking. Bake at 325 degrees Fahrenheit for one hour, and longer if chicken is larger than average size. Test from time to time to see if sufficiently baked.

Chicken in Cream Sauce

To bake chicken in cream sauce, roll the chicken parts in flour with salt and pepper, and then brown them in butter. Combine a cup of sour cream with a cup of water, add sliced mushrooms, and bake the chicken in the sauce.

Deep-fat Fried Chicken

Small fryers of two pounds or less are best for deep-fat frying. Roll the pieces in seasoned flour, and fry for 10 minutes in deep fat at 350 degrees Fahrenheit. Drain before serving.

Broiling Chicken

Broil halves or parts of small broiler-fryers in a pre-heated broiler keeping the skin-side down on the broiler rack. The heat source should be about five inches from the surface of the chicken. Brush the bird with melted butter or margarine, and broil for about 15 minutes. Season and turn. Whole chicken or individual parts weighing about one pound will require 25-30 minutes cooking time.

Roasting Fowl

To roast chicken and small turkeys, place in a 325 degree oven, breast up. Use a shallow, uncovered pan. Protect the breast skin and top of the legs with a loose piece of aluminum. Baste while it is roasting with melted fat. On the average two hours for a three-pound bird is adequate roasting time.

Stewing Chicken

Small pieces of chicken should be covered with boiling water and allowed to simmer. Add seasonings (and vegetables) and cover the kettle. Simmer on low heat for about two hours, and then remove vegetables and add a paste of two tablespoons of flour in cold water for every cup of broth, stirring a bit of the broth in the paste first. While cooking continues over low heat stir until gravy thickens and comes to a boil. Stir for an additional minute and serve.

The Turkey Market

Most turkeys are marketed when young. They are tender-meated and suitable for roasting. Small, very young turkeys that can be broiled or fried as well as roasted, are available in some stores. These will suit the needs of smaller families. Generally, turkeys range from 4 to 24 pounds, ready to cook.

Storing Turkey

Refrigerate your leftover turkey as you would any other fowl. However, if the turkey has been stuffed, first remove the stuffing and store separately.

Carving a Turkey

1. Remove the drumstick by pulling leg from body, loosening it as much as possible. Then cut through skin and soft part of joint. Press knife firmly. If you are hitting bone rather than cartilage at the joint, move the knife to one side or the other until knife can cut through without undue difficulty.

2. Make an incision into the white meat in a horizontal line, parallel to the wing. Cut deeply into the breast until you feel the body frame.

3. Now slice down into the white meat starting halfway up the breast. Cut thick or thin slices to suit your taste. End each downward cut at the horizontal cut first made. Don't carve more than is needed for the meal. Store uncut turkey as a whole. This will keep meat from drying out.

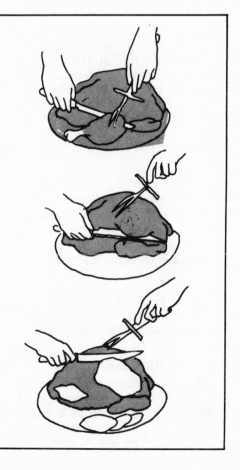

Part Eight

Kitchen Tips on Eggs

Brown vs. White Eggs

In some parts of the country brown eggs are considered to be of a higher quality than white eggs. The reverse is believed to be true in other parts of the country. Actually, there is no difference in the quality, so buy whichever is cheaper.

Raw or Cooked?

If you're not sure whether an egg is raw or cooked, lay it on its side and give it a whirl. If the egg wobbles while rotating, it's raw.

Centering the Yolk

Storing eggs with large end up helps to keep the yolk centered.

Storing Shelled Eggs

A covered container is best for storing whole shelled eggs because the membrane is porous and will absorb the odors of foods stored near them. Egg-whites should be kept in a tightly-covered jar. Yolks keep best covered with water.

No-crack Eggs

A few drops of vinegar added to the water in which eggs are being boiled will keep the shells from cracking and the whites from oozing out.

Eggs in Recipes

The average recipe calls for eggs that are medium to large. If the eggs you are using are small, figure three tablespoons of slightly mixed whole eggs equal one average-sized egg.

Adding Eggs to Batter

It's a good idea not to drop eggs directly from the shell into the batter. One bad egg will spoil the batter. Crack each egg open in a separate bowl. If the egg is rotten you will smell it. Also, if a bit of eggshell falls into it, you will be able to remove it with ease.

Separating Whites and Yolks

There is a way of separating egg-whites and yolks without breaking the yolks. Puncture a small hole in one end of the shell and let the white drain into a dish while the yolk stays unbroken inside. Afterwards, break open the shell and remove the yolk.

Beating Egg Whites

Eggs darken aluminum, so it's a good idea not to beat egg-whites in an aluminum bowl. Use bowls made of stainless-steel, glass, porcelain or enamel.

Boiling Eggs

Sudden temperature changes cause eggshells to crack. So, if you have the time, it is best to start them boiling in cold water. When you do not have time to start the eggs in cold water, run hot water over them for a minute or so.

Using Cracked Shells

If the egg you are about to boil is cracked on one side, crack it a little on the other side. If you do this, you will find that the egg will stay inside the shell while it boils.

Sealing Cracked Eggs

When an eggshell cracks while the egg is being boiled, seal it immediately by adding a splash of vinegar to the boiling water.

Freezing Eggs

Try to avoid freezing foods that contain hard-boiled egg-whites.

Frozen egg-whites change in texture. They become tough and take on a peculiar flavor.

Dried Eggs

Keep dried eggs in unopened packages in a cool place that is about 50-60 degrees Fahrenheit, but preferably in the refrigerator. Once opened, keep in a tightly-covered can or jar in the refrigerator.

fresh egg

old egg –
do not use

Testing the Age of an Egg

If you're in doubt about the freshness of an egg, put it in a deep container of cold water. A fresh egg will lie on its side. An egg that inclines at an angle is several days old. An egg that stands upright is about a week and a half old. An egg that floats to the top is too old to use, and it is wise to throw it out.

Simmering Eggs

It's better to simmer eggs, than boil them, because egg-whites and yolks tend to coagulate at temperatures below the boiling point of water. Simmer soft-cooked eggs three minutes; four minutes for firm but soft yolks; five minutes for eggs even more firm, but still soft. Hard-cooked eggs should be left on the stove for 10 minutes.

If you simmer your hard-cooked eggs, you'll avoid that green division that appears between yolk and white—and you'll avoid that hard-boiled-egg odor. Also, cooking at a high temperature toughens the protein in eggs, and the tougher eggs are, the less appetizing they taste. Eggs cooked at lower temperatures taste better.

Part Nine

Kitchen Tips
on Fruit

Storing Citrus Fruits

Keep your oranges, lemons, limes and grapefruit in the closed bin on the lower shelf of your refrigerator. Place a paper towel under the fruit to absorb excess moisture.

Citrus Fruit Juice

Soak oranges, lemons and limes in a pan of water before squeezing them. Roll the fruit against your countertop to soften the pulp before you cut open the fruit that is about to be squeezed.

That Fresh-Squeezed Taste

There is good reason why canned juice doesn't have the tang of fresh-squeezed. There's something missing. What's missing is the air that was removed during the canning process. Bring canned juice back to life by stirring it well with a spoon, a rotary beater, or in a blender. You can also aerate the juice by pouring it from one container to another several times.

Grated Orange Peel

To improve flavor, grated orange peel can be added to pudding mix or to the batters of cakes and cookies. Grated orange peel not used immediately can be dried out in the oven and stored in tightly-closed containers for future use.

Where the Flavor Is

Whether it's a lemon, a lime, or an orange, the flavor is in the colored (outer) part of the peel (rind). The white part that is next to the actual fruit has a bitter taste. When grating, be careful to avoid this part of the rind.

Storing Bananas

It may sound like an old song but it still holds true: Never store bananas in the refrigerator.

Peeling Peaches

If you soak peaches in boiling water, their skins will come off easily. The same is true for pears.

Making Tastier Fruit Drinks

Cover several pieces of orange and lemon rind with cold water, and bring to a boil. Remove the rind, cool the water. When you add this solution to fruit juices and to fresh fruit drinks, you will enhance the taste considerably.

Storing Strawberries

Strawberries can be stored for several days and still stay firm. To keep them firm, store the berries in a colander so cold air can circulate through them, or keep them uncovered in the box in which they were purchased.

Preparing Fresh Berries

To get the best flavor out of fresh berries, store them in the refrigerator spread out on an open tray. Keep them chilled, but unwashed, until you prepare them for serving. Wash the berries in a colander by running cold water over them. To preserve the flavor, remove the hulls after the berries have been washed.

Serving Fruit

Fresh fruit should be served cold—but not too cold. Take fruit out of the refrigerator at least 15 minutes before serving so that it can warm up slightly.

Thawing Frozen Fruit

If you immerse it in a bowl of room-temperature water, a package of quick-frozen fruit can be thawed ready for serving in a little less than half an hour.

Serving Frozen Fruit

Serve fresh fruit that has been frozen just as soon as it is thawed. When there are still a few icy crystals left, that is when it will taste best.

Baked Apple

To keep apples from bursting out of their skins, prick the skin before putting them in to bake. For added flavor, drop a dried apricot or several raisins into the core area along with the spices.

Cooked Cranberries

The flavor of cooked cranberries can be improved by adding a slice of raw apple to each pint of berries before cooking.

Blanching Almonds

Blanch almonds yourself by pouring boiling water over the shelled nuts. Let them stand in the water until the brown skin has loosened, which usually happens once the water has cooled. To whiten blanched almonds, soak them in cold water and place in the refrigerator.

Toasting Blanched Almonds

For toasting, cut blanched almonds into thin slivers with a sharp knife. Stir the almond slivers in butter melted in a large pie plate. The butter should be just enough to cover the almonds. Bake for 15 minutes in an oven at 350 degrees Fahrenheit—or until they are toasted golden.

Toasting Coconut

You can toast your own packaged or freshly-grated coconut by spreading it in thin layers on a cookie sheet or pan and placing it in an oven at 350 degrees Fahrenheit. Leave it in the oven until it is golden brown, stirring often to be sure it will be toasted evenly.

Dried Fruit

Keep dried fruit in a tightly-covered jar or can, at room temperature, and preferably not above 70 degrees Fahrenheit. In warm, humid weather store in the refrigerator.

Fruit Storage Guide

To get the best flavor from your fruit, use it fresh from the orchard. But if it must be held a few days, follow this storage guide:

Refrigerate: apples, apricots, avocados, berries, cherries, grapes, nectarines, peaches (soft ripe), pears, plums.

Keep at room temperature or refrigerate: grapefruit, lemons, lime, melons, oranges and pineapples.

Keep at room temperature (or slightly cooler): apples (hard), bananas, peaches (firm).

Part Ten

Kitchen Tips on Vegetables

Buy Young Vegetables

Most vegetables should be purchased young, before their starch content has developed. The exceptions include squash and eggplant.

Paring Sparingly

It is better *not* to peel vegetables. But if you *must* peel, pare as close to the skin as possible, because that is where the nutrients are.

Shucking Peas and Beans

Don't shuck more peas or lima beans than you will be serving at the next meal. Store the remainder in their pods.

Boiling Dried Beans and Peas

A quick and effective way to soften dried beans and whole peas is to start by boiling them in water for two minutes. Remove pot from stove, and allow vegetables to soak for one hour. They are now ready to cook.

Softening Dried Beans With Baking Soda

For beans that take an hour or longer to boil, cooking time may be shortened by adding baking soda to the water. With most tap waters, adding ⅛ teaspoon of soda to the water allowed for one cup of dry beans will shorten cooking time about one-fourth. Add to the water at the start. Too much soda will affect flavor and nutritive value, so measure carefully.

Dressing Up Green Beans

Fresh green beans are good with butter. But there is more you can do for occasional variety. Try adding slices of blanched almonds or sauteed mushrooms just before serving. Or, try seasoning with a dash of oregano and onion powder.

Preserving Nutrients

To keep the greatest amount of nutrients in vegetables, boil them in the smallest amount of water possible—and for the shortest time possible. They'll look better—and taste better, and even more important, prepared this way, they are most healthful.

Steaming Vegetables

Steaming vegetables preserves more vitamins and minerals than boiling. Steamers of stainless steel can be purchased for less than five dollars at variety and hardware stores—and are a worthwhile investment.

Vegetable Broth

Don't throw out the water in which vegetables have been cooked. It is rich in vitamins and minerals derived from the cooked vegetables. The liquid makes a refreshing beverage for an in-between-meal snack. Serve it chilled in hot weather, and warm in cold weather. Or, add to recipes that call for water to be added.

Storing Corn on the Cob

Corn on the cob should be stored in its husk. If you will not be serving all in one day, take extra steps to preserve the remaining stalks. Cut a small piece off the stalk and stand each stalk in a pan containing about one inch of water.

Keeping Vegetables Natural

In order to retain the natural color of your vegetables, leave the lid off the pot during the first few minutes of cooking. When steaming or boiling vegetables, add vinegar to the water to improve the color and flavor.

Lower the Flame

It is not necessary to boil vegetables over a high flame. When vegetables begin to cook, turn the heat down a bit. You will be saving on fuel and preserving the nutrients as well.

Uniform Sizes

If you plan to cook whole potatoes, keep the sizes uniform so that all will be done at the same time. The odd sizes can be used for potato salad or other dishes where small pieces are required.

Don't overcook. Potatoes lose their nutritional value if cooked too long.

Preserving Potato Nutrients

Keep the jackets on while boiling potatoes to retain more of the nutrients. The skins of boiled or baked potatoes are very tasty when prepared with melted butter. They are a good source of potassium, which is essential to good health, and which few other foods contain.

To get the greatest nutritional value from potatoes, boil in a minimum of water. This will preserve most of the vitamins.

Keeping Potatoes White

Boiling potatoes in water, with a little milk added, will improve the taste. Milk keeps the potatoes from turning dark, as will a teaspoon of vinegar when added to the water.

Pared potatoes usually retain their whiteness better during boiling than do potatoes cooked in their skins. If potatoes aren't cooked immediately after paring, cover them with water to prevent darkening.

Preparing Potatoes

No matter how potatoes are to be cooked, first remove sprouts and cut off green portions. If potatoes are pared, keep parings thin.

Potatoes slice more easily when the knife is dipped in boiling water first.

Barbecue-baked Potatoes

For tasty, baked potatoes select medium-sized ones. Clean them and wrap in foil. Prick the foil with a fork to allow the steam to escape. Barbecue-bake for an hour or until tender. Open foil and test with a fork from time to time. Serve with plenty of butter and a dash of black pepper.

Over-salted Vegetables

If you find that the vegetables you are cooking have too much salt in the water, throw several pieces of raw potato into the pot and let them boil for a few minutes. The potatoes will absorb much of the excess salt.

Flavoring Canned Vegetables

To restore good flavor to canned vegetables all you need is air. After opening the can, allow to stand for about 15 minutes. The vegetables will pick up oxygen from the atmosphere to replace that which was lost in the canning process— and your vegetables will taste much better.

Acorn and Butternut Squash

Cut the squash lengthwise and take out the seeds. Put a teaspoon of butter in each half, and also a dash of cinnamon and cloves. Bake the squash in a covered pan in an inch of hot water. Preheat the oven and bake for 25 minutes at 400 degrees Fahrenheit. Remove cover, then bake for 10 minutes more, until brown and tender.

Keeping Cauliflower White

Add a piece of lemon to the cauliflower while cooking to keep it from darkening. Overcooking will darken the vegetable, so when it is tender, turn off the heat.

Grating Carrots

To make it easier to grate a carrot, leave on an inch or more of the green top for a handle. Also, remember that the last half-inch of carrot, just beneath the green top, is loaded with vitamins, and should not be thrown away. Keep it for a snack for yourself or the children.

Storing Root Vegetables

Cut off the tops of carrots, beets, turnips and parsnips before storing them. If left on, the tops will draw moisture and food from the roots, and they will cause the vegetable to wilt.

Cucumber Fried in Batter

Cucumber fried in batter tastes somewhat like eggplant fried in batter. Dip the slices in beaten egg, then dip in finely-ground bread crumbs. Fry until golden-brown.

Peas and Pearl Onions

Cook the peas and onions separately; mix and butter them just before serving. Add cream, if you wish, with a sprinkle of your favorite spice to taste.

Onions Without Tears

A one-inch square of bread on the point of your paring knife as you dice or slice an onion will absorb the onion fumes that bring tears to your eyes.

Onion Squeezing

Rub an onion against the finest part of a vegetable grater to extract its juice. It won't take long to produce a teaspoonful. Catch the liquid in a saucer placed beneath the grater.

Running Rice

Boiling rice tends to overflow the pot. A piece of butter added to the water will keep the rice from boiling over. It is important to keep the heat low after boiling has begun. (Adding butter to boiling vegetables will prevent overflowing as well.)

Fluffy Rice

A teaspoon of lemon juice added to the water will keep your rice from becoming lumpy.

Stuffed Peppers and Apples

A stuffed pepper will keep its flavor and its shape if it is baked in a muffin tin. The same holds true for a baked apple.

For Faster Cooking

To shorten cooking time, cut vegetables into pieces: slice, dice, or shred coarsely.

Vegetable Storage Guide

To get the most from your vegetables, the best practice (if possible) is to use them fresh from the orchard. If they must be held a few days, follow this storage guide:

Refrigerate: corn (in husks), peas (in shell).

Refrigerate and keep covered: asparagus, beans (snap or wax), broccoli, cabbage, cauliflower, celery, corn (husked), cucumbers, greens, onions (green), parsley, peas (shelled), peppers (green), radishes.

Refrigerate or keep at room temperature: beets, carrots and squash (summer).

Keep at room temperature (or slightly cooler): onions (dry), potatoes, squash (winter), sweet potatoes, turnips.

Part Eleven

Kitchen Tips on Baked Goods

Storing Bread

. Bread stored at room temperature in a breadbox, or in a similar container, will stay soft, but not for very long. Bread stored in the refrigerator will last longer and will be safe from mold, but it will not stay soft for long.

The best way to store bread is to double-wrap it in moisture-proof paper and to place it in the refrigerator. The double wrapping will keep the moisture in, and the cooler temperature will keep the mold out. If bread is used infrequently, keep it in your freezer, and take out (or cut off) as much as is needed for each day.

Cube Trays for Baking

Metal ice-cube trays no longer needed for making ice can be used in baking. They happen to be an excellent size and shape for molding cakes, especially the long, layered-type of loaf cakes. Since the trays are usually aluminum, they will not rust, and can be used repeatedly.

Saving on Bread

Many stores have a separate section for day-old bread. Although it is sold at reduced prices, it has the same nutritive value as fresh bread, and will keep for as long as a week.

Buy the store's own brand of bread. It is cheaper and, usually, not inferior to the bread supplied by well-known baking companies.

Finally, buy bread by weight, not by size.

Bread Grains

Whole wheat and rye breads have very high nutritional value. Nutritionally they are a much better buy than white breads, and this includes "enriched" white breads.

Soya Bread

Soya flour adds valuable protein content to bread. When baking, use one part soya flour to nine parts of whole wheat flour.

Reheating Baked Goods

Wrap rolls, buns and coffee cakes

in aluminum foil and heat them in an oven at 350 degrees Fahrenheit. Even though they have been re-heated they will still have that fresh-baked flavor. Be careful not to keep them in the oven too long.

To freshen up breads with hard crusts, brush the crusts with some cold water, using a pastry brush if you have one. Place in an oven at 350 degrees Fahrenheit for ten minutes.

Eggs for Baking

If a cake requires two whole eggs and the frosting calls for egg-whites, do a bit of juggling to save eggs. Use one whole egg in the cake plus two egg yolks. The cake will be moist and you will have two egg-whites left for the frosting, instead of two extra egg yolks sitting in the refrigerator.

Baking Biscuits

Biscuits bake best on a flat baking surface (that has no sides). To de-rive the maximum circulation of heat, the baking sheets should be selected so as to allow an inch or two of space between the edges of the sheet and the sides of the oven.

Bread-crumb Boxes

Don't throw away those round salt boxes with the small metal spouts. They can be used again as bread-crumb boxes when the salt has been used up. Pour the finely-ground bread-crumbs down the spout through a funnel.

Old Bread

Don't throw away bread that is too dried out to eat. Allow to stand in the open until it has become hard, and then put it in the oven after you have finished a baking project, and while the oven is still cooling off. Later, convert the bread to crumbs in a blender, or a meat grinder, or by placing them in a paper bag and crushing with a rolling pin. Use the crumbs for meat loaves, croquettes, meat balls, casseroles, and to dip fish before frying or baking.

Long-term Freezing

Yeast rolls, quick breads, cookies and unfrosted cakes and cupcakes, as well as some frosted ones can be frozen for two to three months. With this in mind, you can buy baked goods at special prices, eat them later, and not worry about spoilage.

Keeping Cake Moist

With a toothpick, attach a slice of bread to the cut sides of a circular cake to prevent it from drying out.

Cut a rectangular cake in the middle and serve from the center out. After cutting slices, push ends together to keep the cake fresh.

Oven Circulation

For best baking results, the hot air in the oven must circulate free-ly. To be sure it does, stagger pans on the oven shelves when baking several dishes at the same time.

Chapter Two

CLEANING AND PRESERVING WEARING APPAREL

Part One

Removing Stains and Spots

Introduction

The first part of this chapter discusses the types of products and procedures you should be aware of, and follow, in attempting to remove some of the more unusual types of stains that appear on fabrics.

Testing Stain Removers

Before you use a stain remover, *including water*, test it on an inside hem or pocket so as to be sure that it will not harm the fabric or dye.

Some stain removers damage certain fibers. They may also cause fading or bleeding of dyes, loss of luster, shrinkage, or stretching. They may remove finishes, designs, or pigment prints.

Initial Action

When a staining accident occurs, it is always safe to absorb excess liquid with a clean cloth, a white paper towel, a sponge, or absorbent cotton. Touch the liquid causing the stain with the tip of the absorbent material to avoid forcing the stain further into the fabric. Do not apply pressure to the stained area.

Loosely Woven Fabrics

Loosely woven fabrics, and fabrics woven from low-twist yarns, are likely to suffer yarn slippage if brushed or rubbed while wet.

Acetate Velvet Pile

Velvets with acetate pile should never be treated with a stain remover that contains water. Even the slightest rubbing can damage the matting.

Removing Stains With Chlorine Bleaches

Chlorine bleach is used to remove stains such as catsup, chocolate, syrup, etc. Check the label of bleach to be *sure* that it contains chlorine.

Chlorine bleach damages some fibers, dyes, and finishes. Check the care label for cautions regarding the use of bleach and read the label on the bleach container. Test the fabric in an inconspicuous place before you use bleach on the stain. Do not use chlorine bleach on fabric with a fire-retardant finish unless the care label states that chlorine bleach is safe.

Removing Stains With Ammonia

Ammonia will restore many articles soiled by smoke. It can be used for cleaning glassware, mirrors, enamel-coated items, formica, straw items, and wicker furniture.

Use plain household ammonia. Do not use ammonia with added color or fragrances.

Ammonia changes the color of some dyes. To restore the color, rinse the color-changed area thoroughly with water and apply a few drops of white vinegar. Rinse well with water again.

For use on wool and silk, dilute ammonia with an equal amount of water.

Removing Stains With Alcohol

For removing grass stains or dye stains use rubbing alcohol or denatured alcohol (70-percent or 90-percent concentration). Do not use alcohol with added color or fragrances.

Alcohol will cause some dyes to fade, so test the fabric for color fastness before using alcohol on a stain.

For use on acetate, dilute alcohol with two parts water to one part alcohol.

Removing Stains With Wet Spotter

To remove a variety of stains you will need a wet spotter, and dry spotter.

To prepare wet spotter mix one part glycerine, one part liquid hand-dishwashing detergent, and eight parts water. Shake well before each use.

Cleaning Vinyl Articles

Some vinyl articles are resistant to drycleaning solvents, but many are likely to be damaged by solvents. Drycleaning solvent may remove the plasticizers and cause the garment to stiffen. If removal of an oil or grease stain is attempted, the procedure should consist of very lightly sponging the surface of the vinyl with a cloth barely dampened with drycleaning solvent. Do not make more than a few strokes. Repeated rubbing will remove the plasticizer and may change the appearance of the vinyl surface.

Stain removal procedures using water and liquid detergent with vinegar or ammonia are usually safe on vinyl. Test a hidden hem before trying to remove the stain. A blotting action is the safest method for treating stains on vinyl.

Removing Stains With Peroxide

To remove blood stains or chocolate stains, use the three-percent solution sold as a mild antiseptic. Do not use the stronger solution sold in cosmetic departments for bleaching hair.

Hydrogen peroxide is safe for all fibers, but dyed fabrics should be tested for color fastness.

Store in a cool, dark place. Hydrogen peroxide loses strength when stored for extended periods of time.

Removing Stains With Amyl Acetate

To remove glue or lacquer stains use amyl acetate (banana oil). Ask for "chemically pure amyl acetate" when ordering it in your drug store.

If you cannot obtain amyl acetate, you may substitute fingernail polish remover. Do not use the oily-type nail polish remover.

Amyl acetate is a strong solvent for plastics. Do not allow it to come in contact with plastics or furniture finishes.

Removing Stains With Vinegar

Use white vinegar (colored vinegar can leave a stain) to remove mustard, wax, or jam stains. Vinegar is safe for all fibers, but it changes the color of some dyes. If a dye changes color after vinegar has been used, rinse the color-changed area thoroughly with water, and add a few drops of ammonia. Then, rinse well with water again.

Removing Stains With Dry Spotter

To prepare dry spotter, mix one part coconut oil and eight parts dry-cleaning solvent. This solution is used to remove adhesive tape marks and many other kinds of stains.

Dry spotter keeps well if the container is tightly capped. If you cannot obtain coconut oil, use mineral oil in the same amount as coconut oil.

Removing Stains With an Enzyme Product

You may use either an enzyme pre-soak or an enzyme containing laundry detergent to remove fruit stains, egg-white stains, and others. These products may be stored as purchased, but become active if they are stored after they have been made into a solution.

Adhesive Tape Marks

Marks made by adhesive tape can be removed by applying dry spotter to the stain. Using an absorbent pad, keep the area moist with dry spotter until the stain is removed. When the stain has disappeared, sponge material with water.

If the above procedure is not effective, apply wet spotter, and a few drops of ammonia—again using a pad of absorbent material. Keep the area moist until the stain has disappeared, and then sponge with water.

Removing Stains by Sponging

When directions call for sponging, place the stained area, stained side down, over a pad of absorbent material. Dampen another piece of absorbent material with the stain remover. Sponge the stain lightly, working from the center to the edge. You are less likely to form rings if you keep working out from the center.

Antiperspirant Stains

To remove perspiration stains from washable fabrics soak for 30 minutes in a solution of one quart warm water, ½ teaspoon liquid dishwashing detergent, and one tablespoon ammonia. Rinse with water to remove all ammonia. Soak again in a solution of one quart warm water and one tablespoon vinegar for one hour. Rinse and allow to dry.

If this procedure is not effective, moisten stain with alcohol and blot with an absorbent pad. Flush with water.

Nonwashable fabrics should be treated by applying wet spotter with a few drops of ammonia, and blotting with a moist pad of absorbent material until stain is removed. Remaining traces of stain may be treated with alcohol, as above.

Bleaching with chlorine may be necessary to remove lingering stains caused by perspiration. If so, follow procedure outlined in section on Eye Makeup.

Some have discovered that perspiration stains will disappear from cotton clothing if soaked in salt water for several hours, and then washed out in the usual manner.

Asphalt Stains

Should asphalt come into contact with clothing, apply drycleaning solvent and blot with a moistened pad of absorbent material. Apply dry spotter, again blotting with a moistened pad. Continue alternate soaking in the two solutions until all stain has been removed. Flush with drycleaning solvent and allow to dry.

Blood Stains

Blood stains in washable fabrics should be soaked for 20 minutes in a solution of one quart warm water, ½ teaspoon liquid dishwashing detergent, and one tablespoon ammonia. Then, rinse with water. Stubborn stains can be treated with a laundry detergent containing an enzyme product.

Nonwashable fabrics should be treated by applying wet spotter with a few drops of ammonia, and blotting with a moist pad of absorbent material until stain is removed.

For stains that are not completely removed, wet stain with hydrogen peroxide and add a drop of ammonia. Allow to stand no longer than 15 minutes. Rinse thoroughly with water.

Bathroom Product Stains I

Stains in washable fabrics caused by bath oil, aftershave lotion, mouthwash, or eye drops should be soaked for 20 minutes in a solution of one quart warm water, ½ teaspoon liquid dishwashing detergent, and one tablespoon ammonia. Then, rinse with water. Stubborn stains can be treated with a laundry detergent containing an enzyme product.

Nonwashable fabrics should be

treated by applying wet spotter with a few drops of ammonia, and blotting with a moist pad of absorbent material until stain is removed.

Bathroom Product Stains II

Remove stains caused by toothpaste, shaving cream, suntan lotion, and home permanent solutions by soaking washables for 15 minutes in a solution of one quart warm water, ½ teaspoon liquid detergent, and one tablespoon vinegar. Rinse with water. Stubborn stains can be treated with a laundry detergent containing an enzyme product.

Nonwashable fabrics should be treated by applying wet spotter with a few drops of vinegar, and blotting with a moist pad of absorbent material until stain is removed.

Bleaching with chlorine may be necessary to remove lingering stains caused by suntan lotion. If so, follow procedure outlined in section on Eye Makeup.

Calamine Lotion Stains

Stains caused by calamine lotion may be removed by applying dry spotter to the stain. Using an absorbent pad, keep the area moist with dry spotter until the stain is removed. When stain has disappeared, sponge material with water.

If the above procedure is not effective, apply wet spotter, and a few drops of ammonia, again using a pad of absorbent material. Keep area moist until stain is removed. When stain has disappeared, sponge material with water.

Cooking Oil Stains

For heavy stains caused by all types of cooking oil, apply drycleaning solvent and blot with a moistened pad of absorbent material. Apply dry spotter, again blotting with a moistened pad. Continue alternate soaking in the two solutions until all stain has been removed. Flush with drycleaning solvent and allow to dry.

Beverage Stains

Stains caused by coffee, tea, soft drinks, and alcoholic beverages such as wine, whiskey, beer, and cordials are easily removed by the following method:

Soak washable fabrics for 15 minutes in a solution of one quart warm water, ½ teaspoon liquid dishwashing detergent, and one tablespoon vinegar. Rinse with water. Stubborn stains can be treated with a laundry detergent containing an enzyme product.

Nonwashable fabrics should be treated by applying wet spotter with a few drops of vinegar, and blotting with a moist pad of absorbent material until stain is removed.

With the exception of beer, bleaching may be necessary to remove traces of stain from garments. If so, follow procedure described at the end of section on Eye Makeup.

Coffee stains (if cream and sugar have *not* been added) can be removed by placing a liberal dose of club soda on the area and rubbing lightly with a rag.

Carbon Paper Stains

Garments soiled by carbon paper, carbon typewriting ribbon, mimeograph ink, or correction fluid can be cleaned by applying dry spotter to stain and blotting with a pad of absorbent material until stain is removed. Flush with drycleaning solvent.

If the above procedure is not effective, apply amyl acetate (banana oil) to the stain and blot with a pad of absorbent material. Allow to stand for 15 minutes, then flush with drycleaning solvent.

Bleaching with chlorine may be necessary if traces of stain remain on the fabric. If so, follow procedure outlined in section on Eye Makeup.

Crayon Stains

Crayon marks caused by a wax or grease crayon can be removed by applying dry spotter to the stain. Using an absorbent pad, keep the area moist with dry spotter until the stain is removed. When stain has disappeared, sponge material with water.

If the above procedure is not effective, apply wet spotter, and a few drops of ammonia, again using a pad of absorbent material. Keep area moist until stain is removed. When stain has disappeared, sponge material with water.

Wax crayon on carpets can be removed by covering the damaged area with paper toweling and ironing the towel with a warm iron. The wax will melt and be absorbed by the towel.

Crayon marks on a painted wall can be erased by dabbing fingernail polish remover on a clean cloth and rubbing the area.

Egg-White Stains

Washable fabrics soiled by egg-white should be soaked for 20 minutes in a solution of one quart warm water, ½ teaspoon liquid detergent, and one tablespoon am-

Chocolate Stains

Chocolate stains may require special treatment in addition to the procedures outlined below. Begin by applying dry spotter to the stain. Using an absorbent pad, keep the area moist with dry spotter until the stain is removed. When stain has disappeared, sponge material with water.

If the above procedure is not effective, apply a few drops of liquid handwashing detergent and a few drops of ammonia, again using a pad of absorbent material. Keep area moist until stain is removed. When stain has disappeared,

sponge material with water. Stubborn stains can be treated with a detergent containing an enzyme product.

Bleaching with chlorine may be necessary to remove lingering stains caused by chocolate. If so, follow procedure outlined in section on Eye Makeup.

If above remedies fail, try bleaching chocolate stains with hydrogen peroxide. Keep the area moist with peroxide, and a drop or two of ammonia, for up to 15 minutes. Rinse with water.

monia. Then, rinse with water. Stubborn stains can be treated with a laundry detergent containing an enzyme product.

Nonwashable fabrics should be treated by applying wet spotter with a few drops of ammonia, and blotting with a moist pad of absorbent material until stain is removed.

Red and Yellow Dye Stains

Fabric stains caused by *red* dye can be caused by food coloring, hair dye, fabric dye, red ink, mercurochrome, or water color paint. *Yellow* stains may result from using products which contain a derivative of picric acid. To remove, washable fabrics should be soaked for 30 minutes in a solution of one quart warm water, ½ teaspoon liquid dishwashing detergent, and one tablespoon ammonia. Rinse with water to remove all ammonia. Soak in a solution of one quart warm water and one tablespoon vinegar for one hour. Rinse and allow to dry. If this procedure is not effective, moisten stain with alcohol and blot with an absorbent pad. Flush with water.

Nonwashable fabrics should be treated by applying wet spotter with a few drops of ammonia, and blotting with a moist pad of absorbent material until stain is removed. Remaining traces of stain may be treated with alcohol, as above.

Bleaching with chlorine may be necessary to remove lingering stains caused by red dye. If so, follow procedure outlined in section on Eye Makeup.

Dairy Products Stains

Milk, cream, ice cream, egg-yolk and cheese are among the culprits here. Apply dry spotter to the stain. Using an absorbent pad, keep the area moist with dry spotter until the stain is removed. When stain had disappeared, sponge material with water.

If the above procedure is not effective, apply a few drops of liquid handwashing detergent and a few drops of ammonia, again using a pad of absorbent material. Keep area moist until stain has disappeared and then sponge with water. Stubborn stains can be treated with a detergent containing an enzyme product.

Bleaching with chlorine may be necessary to remove lingering stains caused by cheese. If so, follow procedure outlined in section on Eye Makeup.

Fish Glue Stains

In washable fabrics, hard-to-remove stains caused by decaying fish compounds (such as the dilute fish emulsion used as plant food), should be soaked for 20 minutes in a solution of one quart warm water, ½ teaspoon liquid dishwashing detergent, and one tablespoon ammonia. Then, rinse with water. Stubborn stains can be treated with a laundry detergent containing an enzyme product.

Nonwashable fabrics should be treated by applying wet spotter with a few drops of ammonia, and blotting with a moist pad of absorbent material until stain is removed.

Additional Dye Stains

Most dyes are meant to be permanent and are difficult to remove. For all dye stains *except* those caused by red and yellow dyes, try the following.

Soak washable fabrics for 30 minutes in a solution of one quart warm water, ½ teaspoon liquid dishwashing detergent, and one tablespoon vinegar. Rinse with water. Moisten stain with alcohol and blot with an absorbent pad, then flush with alcohol. Soak for an additional 30 minutes in a solution of one quart warm water, ½ teaspoon liquid dishwashing detergent, and one tablespoon ammonia. Rinse with water.

Nonwashable fabrics should be treated by applying wet spotter with a few drops of vinegar, and blotting with a moist pad of absorbent material. Flush with water and treat with alcohol, as above. Wet spotter with a few drops of ammonia may be applied to stubborn stains.

The above method works well for stains caused by fabric dye, food coloring, bluing, gentian violet, ink, hair dye, shoe dye, and water color paint. If traces of stain remain, use chlorine bleach, and follow the procedure outlined in section on Eye Makeup.

Catsup Stains

Hard-to-remove stains caused by catsup and steak or chili sauce are best dealt with by applying dry spotter to the stain. Using an absorbent pad, keep the area moist with dry spotter until the stain is removed. When stain has disappeared, sponge material with water.

If the above procedure is not effective, apply a few drops of liquid detergent and a few drops of ammonia, again using a pad of absorbent material. Keep area moist until stain is removed. When stain has disappeared, sponge material with water. Stubborn stains can be treated with a detergent containing an enzyme product.

Bleaching with chlorine may be necessary to remove lingering stains caused by catsup and steak or chili sauce. If so, follow procedure outlined in section on Eye Makeup.

Chewing Gum Stains

Peanut butter rubbed in hair matted with chewing gum removes the gum. Follow this by removing the peanut butter with a spot shampoo.

Face Makeup Stains

Face powder, lipstick, rouge, or makeup of the liquid or pancake variety may cause stains around the neck of garments. These are best removed by applying dry spotter to the stain. Using an absorbent pad, keep the area moist with dry spotter until the stain is removed. When stain has disappeared, sponge material with water.

If the above procedure is not effective, apply wet spotter, and a few drops of ammonia, again using a pad of absorbent material. Keep area moist until stain is removed, and then sponge material with water.

Eye Makeup Stains

Fabric soiled by eyebrow pencil, eyeliner, eye shadow, mascara, or any similar type of eye makeup, may be cleaned by applying dry spotter to the stain until the stain is removed. Then, sponge material with water.

If the above procedure is not effective, apply wet spotter, and a few drops of ammonia, again using a pad of absorbent material. Keep area moist until stain is gone and then sponge material with water.

To remove the final traces of stain caused by eye makeup, use a solution of one teaspoon chlorine bleach to one teaspoon water. Apply with a dropper for no longer than *two* minutes. Flush with water, apply one teaspoon of vinegar to the stain, and flush with water again.

Cake Frosting Stains

Smudges caused by cake frosting can be removed by applying dry spotter to the stain. Using an absorbent pad, keep the area moist with dry spotter until the stain is removed. When the stain has disappeared, sponge material with water.

If the above procedure is not effective, apply a few drops of liquid handwashing detergent and a few drops of ammonia, again using a pad of absorbent material. Keep area moist until stain is removed. When stain has disappeared, sponge material with water. Stubborn stains can be treated with a detergent containing an enzyme product.

Syrup Stains

Corn or maple syrup, molasses, cough syrup, and caramelized sugar can be the cause of bothersome stains. Soak washables for 15 minutes in a solution of one quart warm water, ½ teaspoon liquid dishwashing detergent, and one tablespoon vinegar. Rinse with water. Stubborn stains can be treated with a laundry detergent containing an enzyme product.

Nonwashable fabrics should be treated by applying wet spotter with a few drops of vinegar, and blotting with a moist pad of absorbent material until stain is removed.

Bleaching with chlorine may be necessary to remove lingering stains caused by caramelized sugar. If so, follow procedure outlined in section on Eye Makeup.

Fruit and Vegetable Stains

The juice from various types of fruits and vegetables may cause stains on fabrics. Soak washables for 15 minutes in a solution of one quart warm water, ½ teaspoon liquid dishwashing detergent, and one tablespoon vinegar. Rinse with water. Stubborn stains can be treated with a laundry detergent containing an enzyme product.

Nonwashable fabrics should be treated by applying wet spotter with a few drops of vinegar, and blotting with a moist pad of absorbent material until stain is removed.

Bleaching with chlorine may be necessary to remove lingering stains caused by vegetables. If so, follow procedure outlined at end of section on Eye Makeup.

Glue Stains

For stains caused by mucilage, airplane glue, plastic glue, liquid solder, and plastic cement, apply dry spotter to stain and blot with a pad of absorbent material until stain is removed. Flush with drycleaning solvent.

If the above procedure is not effective, apply amyl acetate (banana oil) to the stain and blot with a pad of absorbent material. Allow to stand for 15 minutes, then flush with drycleaning solvent.

Grass Stains

To remove grass stains, sponge garment with drycleaning solvent and allow to dry. Then blot with a pad of absorbent material moistened with amyl acetate. Flush with drycleaning solvent and allow to dry.

If the above procedure is not effective, sponge fabric with water. Apply wet spotter and a small amount of vinegar. Flush with water
and allow to dry.

Rubbing the fabric with a pad moistened in alcohol may be necessary to remove lingering traces of stain.

Grease Stains

Most types of grease used in cooking (i.e., lard, margarine), or lubricating oils, salves, and ointments used in the home may be removed by applying dry spotter to the stain. Using an absorbent pad, keep the area moist with dry spotter until the stain has disappeared, and then sponge with water.

If the above procedure is not effective, apply wet spotter, and a few drops of ammonia, again using a pad of absorbent material. Keep area moist until stain is removed. When stain has disappeared, sponge material with water.

Grease Stains on Wallpaper I

Place a piece of blotting paper over the stained wallpaper as soon as you notice it. Press an iron at medium heat against the blotting paper (using wool setting). The grease will be liquefied by the heat and absorbed by the blotting paper. You may have to make several tries to get up all the stain. Use a clean

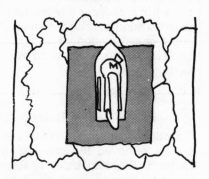

section of the blotting paper each time. If you have acted quickly enough, the soil will disappear.

Grease Stains on Wallpaper II

Place a paste made of cornstarch and water on the grease spot and leave it there until it dries. When it is dry, brush it off and the stain should disappear. If this does not work try again with a paste of fuller's earth and carbon tetrachloride. Both can be purchased at paint and hardware stores.

Grease Stains on Polyester

Grease stains on polyester garments can be rubbed with talcum

powder. Use your fingertips. Allow the powder to stand for 24 hours, then brush off. Repeat procedure if necessary.

Hair Spray Stains

The sticky residue left by hair spray on fabric surfaces can be removed by applying dry spotter to the stain. Using an absorbent pad, keep the area moist with dry spotter until the stain has disappeared, and then sponge with water.

If the above procedure is not effective, apply wet spotter, and a few drops of ammonia, again using a pad of absorbent material. Keep area moist until stain is removed. When stain has disappeared, sponge material with water.

Hand Lotion Stains

Hand lotion can cause troublesome staining when brought into contact with sheer or delicate fabrics. To remove, apply dry spotter to the stain. Using an absorbent pad, keep the area moist with dry spotter. When stain has disappeared, sponge material with water.

If the above procedure is not effective, apply wet spotter, and a few drops of ammonia, again using a pad of absorbent material. Keep area moist until stain is removed. When stain has disappeared, sponge material with water.

India Ink Stains

India ink stains are most effectively dealt with by applying dry spotter to the stain. Using an absorbent pad, keep the area moist with dry spotter. When stain has disappeared, sponge material with water.

If the above procedure is not effective, apply wet spotter, and a few drops of ammonia, again using a pad of absorbent material. Keep area moist until stain is removed, and then sponge with water.

Jams and Jellies Stains

Children's clothing is often soiled by sticky jams, jellies, fruit preserves, and fruit juices. Remove stains from washables by soaking for 15 minutes in a solution of one quart warm water, ½ teaspoon liquid dishwashing detergent, and one tablespoon vinegar. Rinse with water. Stubborn stains can be treated with a laundry detergent containing an enzyme product.

Nonwashable fabrics should be treated by applying wet spotter with a few drops of vinegar, and blotting with a moist pad of absorbent material until stain is removed.

Bleaching with chlorine may be necessary to remove lingering stains. If so, follow procedure outlined at end of section on Eye Make-up.

Marking Pen Stains

Clothing stains caused by felt-tip marker ink can be removed by applying dry spotter to the stain. Using an absorbent pad, keep the area moist with dry spotter. When stain has disappeared, sponge material with water.

If the above procedure is not effective, apply wet spotter, and a few drops of ammonia, again using a pad of absorbent material. Keep area moist, and when stain has disappeared, sponge material with water.

To remove the final traces of stain caused by felt-tip marker ink, use a solution of one teaspoon chlorine bleach to one teaspoon water. Apply with a dropper for no longer than *two* minutes. Flush with water, apply one teaspoon of vinegar to the stain, and flush with water again.

Mustard Stains

Mustard stains should be treated by placing the stain on a smooth surface and carefully scraping off excess mustard. Then, flush with drycleaning solvent, and allow to dry. Follow this by sponging the fabric with water, applying wet spotter and vinegar, and then flushing again with water.

If this does not remove the stain, apply hydrogen peroxide and a drop of vinegar, and allow to stand for 15 minutes. Flush with water and allow to dry.

Nose Drops Stains

Fabric stains caused by nose drops can be removed by applying dry spotter to the stain. Using an absorbent pad, keep the area moist with dry spotter until the stain is removed, and then sponge material with water.

If the above procedure is not effective, apply wet spotter, and a few drops of ammonia, again using a pad of absorbent material. Keep area moist. When stain has disappeared, sponge material with water.

Rubber Cement

Rubber cement can be removed by applying drycleaning solvent and blotting with a moistened pad of absorbent material. Apply dry spotter, again blotting with a moistened pad. Continue alternate soaking in the two solutions until all stain has been removed. Flush with drycleaning solvent and allow to dry.

Mud Stains

Ground-in dirt in children's playclothes is a perennial problem. Soak washables for 15 minutes in a solution of one quart warm water, ½ teaspoon liquid detergent, and one tablespoon vinegar. Rinse with water. Stubborn stains can be treated with a laundry detergent containing an enzyme product.

Nonwashable fabrics should be treated by applying wet spotter with a few drops of vinegar, and blotting with a moist pad of absorbent material until stain is removed.

Bleaching with chlorine may be necessary to remove lingering stains caused by mud and dirt. If so, follow procedure outlined at end of section on Eye Makeup.

Lacquer Stains

Stains resulting from contact with lacquer, varnish, and fingernail polish or nail hardener, can be treated by applying dry spotter to stain and blotting with a pad of absorbent material until stain is removed. Flush with drycleaning solvent.

If the above procedure is not effective, apply amyl acetate to stain and blot with a pad of absorbent material. Allow to stand for 15 minutes, then flush with drycleaning solvent.

Insecticide Stains

A special problem during the summer months, insecticide stains on clothing can be treated by applying dry spotter to the stain. Using an absorbent pad, keep the area moist with dry spotter until the stain is removed. When stain has disappeared, sponge material with water.

If the above procedure is not effective, apply wet spotter, and a few drops of ammonia, again using a pad of absorbent material. Keep area moist until stain is removed. When stain has disappeared, sponge with water.

Meat Soup

Greasy stains caused by soups containing meat can be treated in the following manner. Washable fabrics should be soaked for 20 minutes in a solution of one quart warm water, ½ teaspoon liquid dishwashing detergent, and one tablespoon ammonia. Then, rinse with water. Stubborn stains can be treated with a laundry detergent containing an enzyme product.

Nonwashable fabrics should be treated by applying wet spotter with a few drops of ammonia, and blotting with a moist pad of absorbent material until stain is removed.

Mucus Stains

Washable fabrics soiled by mucus or vomit can be cleaned by soaking for 20 minutes in a solution of one quart warm water, ½ teaspoon liquid detergent, and one tablespoon ammonia. Then, rinse with water. Stubborn stains can be treated with a laundry detergent containing an enzyme product. Uric acid stains can also be removed by this method.

Nonwashable fabrics should be treated by applying wet spotter with a few drops of ammonia, and blotting with a moist pad of absorbent material until stain is removed.

Soups and Sauces Stains

For fabric soiled by gravy, mayonnaise, soup, or salad dressing, apply dry spotter to the stain. Using an absorbent pad, keep the area moist with dry spotter until the stain is removed. When stain has disappeared, sponge material with water.

If the above procedure is not effective, apply a few drops of liquid dishwashing detergent and a few drops of ammonia, again using a pad of absorbent material. Keep area moist until stain is removed. When stain has disappeared, sponge material with water. Stubborn stains can be treated with a detergent containing an enzyme product.

Starch Stains

In washable fabrics, stains caused by too much starch should be soaked for 20 minutes in a solution of one quart warm water, ½ teaspoon liquid dishwashing detergent, and one tablespoon ammonia. Then, rinse with water. Stubborn stains can be treated with a laundry detergent containing an enzyme product.

Nonwashable fabrics should be treated by applying wet spotter with a few drops of ammonia, and blotting with a moist pad of absorbent material until stain is removed.

Removing Stains by Spooning

The bowl of a smooth stainless steel teaspoon is an effective tool for loosening stains.

Place the stain directly on the working surface without any absorbent material underneath. Add the stain remover.

Move the bowl of the spoon back and forth about ¼ inch in each direction. Short strokes are the most effective. Do not press down with the spoon. This may damage the fabric.

Do not use this procedure on delicate fabrics.

Tar Stains

Tar stains on clothing may appear hopeless, but will usually yield to an application of dry spotter. Using an absorbent pad, keep the area moist with dry spotter until the stain is removed, and then sponge material with water.

If the above procedure is not effective, apply wet spotter, and a few drops of ammonia, again using a pad of absorbent material. Keep area moist until stain is removed. When stain has disappeared, sponge material with water.

Tobacco Stains

Tobacco stains can be removed by soaking washables for 15 minutes in a solution of one quart warm water, ½ teaspoon liquid dishwashing detergent, and one tablespoon vinegar. Rinse with water. Stubborn stains can be treated with a laundry detergent containing an enzyme product.

Nonwashable fabrics should be treated by applying wet spotter with a few drops of vinegar, and blotting with a moist pad of absorbent material until stain is removed.

Bleaching with chlorine may be necessary to remove lingering stains caused by tobacco. If so, follow procedure outlined in section on Eye Makeup.

Water Stains

To remove water stains, dip a soft cotton cloth in some spirits of camphor and rub well. Or, if you prefer, prepare a solution of one part ammonia, one part turpentine, and one part linseed oil—stir thoroughly and then apply to the stained area. This latter solution is also recommended for wooden surfaces.

Wax and Polish Stains

To remove fabric stains caused by floor wax, furniture polish, or shoe polish, apply dry spotter to the stain. Using an absorbent pad, keep the area moist with dry spotter, and when stain has disappeared, sponge material with water.

If the above procedure is not effective, apply wet spotter, and a few drops of ammonia, again using a pad of absorbent material. Keep area moist until the stain has disappeared. Sponge material with water.

To remove the final traces of stain caused by wax and polish, use a solution of one teaspoon chlorine bleach to one teaspoon water. Apply with a dropper for no longer than *two* minutes. Flush with water, apply one teaspoon of vinegar to the stain, and flush with water again.

Part Two

Care and Maintenance of Clothing

● ●

Prevent Running

To prevent colored fabrics from running, soak the garments first in cold water to which vinegar has been added. Then, wash in the usual manner.

Removing Sweater Fuzz

To remove fuzz from sweaters and other knitted garments, pull garment tight over an ironing board. Shave surface lightly with safety razor, or use sandpaper.

Lint Catcher

To prevent lint from being picked up from other garments, place several large pieces of nylon net in your dryer along with the dark clothes and blankets that are being dried. The nylon net acts like a whisk broom.

Wrinkled Clothes I

If you hang your clothes on hangers while the garments still retain your body heat, wrinkles will fall away more quickly.

Wrinkled Clothes II

Wrinkled wool and wool mixture suits that do not appear badly wrinkled when first unpacked can usually be worn immediately because most of the wrinkles will disappear in about an hour.

Wrinkled Clothes III

Put a terry cloth towel, dampened with water, in the closet with newly unpacked clothes and close the door. In a few hours most of the wrinkles will disappear. Before hanging, you should give the clothing a thorough shaking.

Removing Hairs

Trying to remove animal hair or lint from your clothing with a whisk broom is an almost impossible task. One effective method of solving this problem is to use adhesive tape or a piece of moistened masking tape. Press the sticky side lightly against the surface of the clothing several times and you will succeed in picking up all the lint and hairs.

Clothes Hangers

If you are short on wooden or heavy-duty plastic hangers, hang your garments on *two* wire hangers placed together for the added strength required.

Reviving Sports Jerseys

An old sports jersey that has been outgrown is still of some use. Sew up the neck and sleeves and stuff it with old rags, and sew up the open ends. It will serve as a good knock-around pillow for a youngster's room.

Short Blankets

If your blankets have shrunk, you can lengthen them by sewing a strip of muslin of a complementary color to the unseen end of the blanket—the end that will be tucked in at the foot of the bed.

Thicker is Warmer

The thicker a blanket, the warmer it will be. Test the nap of a wool blanket by giving it a squeeze, then releasing it; the nap should spring back.

The heavier the sheet, the longer it will wear. Heavy muslin sheets will last longer and not tear as easily as those of medium weight.

Wooden Hangers

Some wooden hangers are rough and cause damage to clothes. To keep wooden hangers from snagging clothing, run sandpaper over them lightly, and then coat them with clear shellac.

Garment Bags

Make your own garment bag to protect suits and dresses by slitting old pillow cases at the sewn end just enough to pull them over hangers holding the garments.

Electric Blankets

Make an electric blanket for a king-size bed by sewing together two twin-size electric blankets. Not only will this cost about 20% less than buying a king-size electric blanket, it will offer dual control of heat.

Mending Garments

There is no need to throw away a torn garment you would really like to wear again. Most tears can be fixed with a piece of mending tape applied to the reverse side of the garment. Apply the patch with a medium hot iron.

If you have no mending tape handy, any piece of fabric similar in texture and coloring to the torn cloth will serve the purpose. Simply apply any type of transparent wood glue to the fabric and press into position with a heated iron until the fabrics bond. The effect will be a permanent repair that is hard to detect. Although it will be stiffer than a patch that has been sewn on, it will take much less time than needlework.

Storing Lace

To keep lace looking better and lasting longer, store lace articles in waxed paper. It will help keep the threads from rotting.

Storing Fur

Fur stored in humidified closets will look better and last longer. You can make your own humidifier by placing a bowl of water with a sponge in it in the closet. Add water periodically to replace the water that has evaporated.

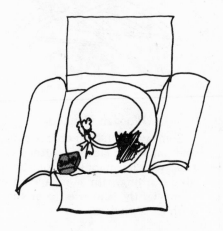

Keeping Hats White

To retard a white hat from yellowing, store it in a box with a small piece of ordinary yellow soap and/or black tissue paper. Even white coats can be kept whiter if stored in a box in this way.

Suede Saver

When sudsing and washing suede synthetics by hand, do not squeeze or wring the garments. To remove excess moisture, roll the clothing in a towel. Then lay flat or hang to dry.

Suede Gloves

To freshen suede gloves, put the gloves on your hands and rub them with a slice of stale bread. Use thick slices if you can. When the bread appears to be sufficiently soiled, take another slice and repeat the process.

Mildew on Fabrics

Fabric on your furniture and luggage can be restored, if you will sponge it with denatured alcohol and water, mixed in equal parts. Then, allow to dry in fresh air, if possible. The musty odor should disappear.

Yellowed Fur

A number of white furs have been bleached before you buy them. In time, the oxygen in the air turns the fur yellow. Re-bleach the fur by spraying it with a hydrogen peroxide solution. Hanging the fur in the sun after the spraying sometimes speeds up the bleaching process. Brushing with soft bristles may also remove some of the yellowing.

Damp Closet Cures

Clothing stored in damp closets is apt to be smelly and subject to mildew. One cure is proper ventilation. You can either leave the closet door open for several hours a day, or you can replace the old door with a louvre door.

Another solution is to provide some heat to remove the dampness. It can be provided by keeping a 60-watt electric bulb burning in the closet at all times.

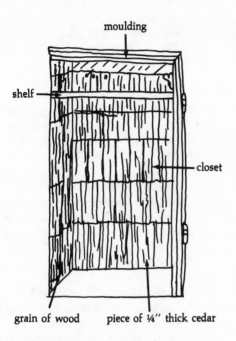

moulding

shelf

closet

grain of wood   piece of ¼" thick cedar

Mothproofing a Closet

Clothes closets can be made mothproof by lining the walls with thin pieces of cedar. Try to locate pieces that are ¼-inch thick. The wood has a strong fragrance that repels moths. Attach with nails or glue to your closet walls.

On Buying Shoes

The best time to buy shoes is late in the afternoon. By that time your feet will have expanded. This is especially true in hot weather. If you buy shoes in the morning, they are likely to pinch your feet in the afternoon.

Also, it is good to remember that since one foot is usually larger than the other, it is wise to make sure the shoes you buy fit the *larger* foot comfortably.

New Shoes

Put some polish on your new shoes before you wear them for the first time. The wax protection will get them off to a good start. Also, if you wish to add years of good wear to your shoes, polish them frequently. This will keep the leather fresh and soft.

Changing Shoes

Double the life of your shoes by changing them daily. Shoes need air to keep them fresh and for all the perspiration that collects in them to be dissipated. By giving your shoes a day of rest you are also slowing the deterioration process that eventually affects leather products.

Patent Leather Shoes

Cold weather often affects patent leather shoes, causing them to crack. You can protect against this by applying a slight film of petroleum jelly to the shoes. Then, polish with a clean cloth.

Kid Shoes

Ordinary cleaning fluid will remove stains from kid shoes, as will ordinary cuticle remover. Moisten a cloth with either product and rub the soiled spots. They should disappear quickly.

Kid Slippers

Gold and silver kid slippers tarnish when allowed to be exposed to the air for prolonged periods. When you are not wearing them, wrap them in black tissue paper or some other dark material, and store them in a box.

Cleaning Patent Leather

To clean patent leather, one easy solution is to saturate a clean rag with orange juice and rub well until all blemishes disappear.

Slippery Soles

Slippery soles are dangerous. You can correct the problem by sandpapering them and by rubbing

on linseed oil. It is especially important to take these steps to keep your child from slipping.

Suede Shoes I

To keep your suede shoes looking good, rub them with a dry sponge after each wearing. Rubbing them with a piece of stale rye bread has also proven to keep suede shoes in good condition.

Suede Shoes II

Another method of keeping suede shoes in condition is to first remove all dust and dirt particles. Then hold the shoes, one at a time, over a pot of boiling water or some other source of steam. When the nap has been raised, stroke the raised nap with a soft brush, and allow the shoes to dry thoroughly before wearing them.

Rain Spots on Suede

A good way of removing stains on suede shoes, hats, and handbags is to brush the surfaces gently with an emery board.

Lemon Juice for Shoes

An effective way of giving leather a high shine is to place a few drops of lemon juice on a rag and to rub well into the leather.

Shoe Polish Applicator

One of the softest applicators you can find for shoe polish is a powder puff. If you decide to use a puff instead of a brush make sure it is new and clean.

A Substitute Shoe Polish

In an emergency, floor wax can be used as shoe polish. Since floor wax is neutral in color, it can be used on light or dark-colored shoes.

Touching up Scuffed Shoes

Black acrylic paint or paint used to touch-up cars is useful in restoring badly scuffed shoes. A wax crayon of the same color can also do a good job.

Shoe Eyelets

Metal eyelets on shoes often become discolored as a result of the pressure exerted on them by the shoelaces. You can prevent this discoloration by coating the eyelets with shellac which is colorless.

Darkening Leather Goods

Light-tan leather shoes and belts can be darkened by rubbing them with a cloth dipped in ammonia. Apply the ammonia uniformly for an even finish.

Opening a Shoe Polish Can

If you are among those who are always looking for a coin (or similar object) to pry open your shoe polish can, you can solve this problem easily. Simply select a washer of the correct thickness. Screw it to the handle-end of your polishing brush so that it protrudes about ¼ inch.

Cleaning Shoebrushes

From time to time shoebrushes must be cleaned. Soak them for ½ hour in warm, sudsy water to which a few drops of turpentine have been added. After soaking, hang up to drip off and dry.

Squeaky Shoes

Silence your squeaky shoes by punching small holes in the sole with an ice pick. The best spot is right behind the ball of the foot. Of course, this should be done only with shoes that would otherwise be unusable.

Shoes for Travel

Don't throw away your old socks, because they are extremely useful as shoe mittens. When packing your bag for a trip, insert each shoe in a sock and avoid dirtying the rest of the clothes in your suitcase.

before : after

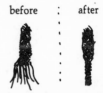

Frayed Shoestrings

When the metal tips come off shoestrings, the material frays quickly. To prevent fraying, dip the ends in hot paraffin, twist, and allow them to dry thoroughly. Dipping the ends of the shoestrings in nail polish is also an effective way of preventing the ends from separating.

Restoring Rain-soaked Shoes

Shoes that have become rain-soaked take two days to dry, and the leather will be stiff and hard. If you want to restore wet shoes, clean them with saddle soap while they are still damp and let the soap remain on them while they dry. Remove the dried soap with a slightly damp soft cloth in 48 hours.

If the shoes are very wet, stuff them with paper toweling to preserve their shape.

Hardened Shoe Polish

Hardened shoe polish can be softened with a little turpentine. Another way of softening shoe polish is by heating the metal container in a pot of hot water.

Chapter Three

CLEANING
AND
PRESERVING
HOUSEHOLD
INTERIORS

Part One

Floors, Walls, Ceilings, and Woodwork

Removing Old Floor Wax

To remove old wax on your floor, you don't need a special wax remover. Powdered detergent and ammonia will work just as well. Use ¾ cup of detergent and 1/3 cup of household ammonia per gallon of warm water. Spread the solution on the floor for three to five minutes, then rub it off with a coarse-textured cleaning cloth. You may have to use a scrub-brush to get at stubborn spots. Rinse with clean warm water.

Built-up Floor Wax

Stubborn patches of built-up floor wax or dirt can be removed by rubbing with fine steel wool, moistened with a little turpentine.

Removing Stains From Carpets

Spot stains can be removed from carpets easily if you clean them immediately after they occur. First, wipe the surface with a cloth or blot with a paper towel. Apply dry-cleaning fluid, working from the edge of the stain toward the center. Use a gentle blotting motion. If this is ineffective, mix one teaspoon detergent and one teaspoon white vinegar with one quart of water, and apply to the stain. Allow to dry and then brush the pile.

Odor From Pets

Spread salt over the damp spot where a pet has soiled your carpet. If the spot has already dried, add water to the salt. Leave a thick paste of salt on the spot for a day, and then remove by vacuuming. Be sure to empty the vacuum bag immediately and clean any of the vacuum parts that may have come in contact with the salt.

Curling Throw-rugs

Throw-rugs lose their attractiveness when their edges begin to curl—and they are also a source of accidents. Avoid the problem by dipping the ends of freshly washed rugs in weak starch. Dry them thoroughly before putting them back on the floor.

Eliminating Paint Odors

Believe it or not, an onion cut in half and placed in a large open pan of cold water will absorb the odor of fresh paint in a matter of hours. Use a large onion for best results.

Restoring Shellacked Floors

Shellacked floors, like all others, wear along the path of greatest traffic. Such paths can be quickly restored by rubbing them with a rag soaked in alcohol. Make sweeping strokes with the rag so that you bring dissolved shellac from the less worn adjacent sides into the path. You can also brush on *new* shellac which has been diluted with an equal amount of alcohol (one cup of shellac to one cup of alcohol).

Slippery Rugs

To prevent a rug from sliding around on hardwood floors, sew or glue a rubber ring to each corner of the rug, and the rug will stay in place.

Frayed Rugs

If you do not want to go to the trouble or expense of rebinding a rug that has frayed edges, trim off the straggly threads with a shears or a razor. Select a glue that is transparent, place a bead of glue along the entire edge. When it hardens, your rug or carpet will hold up well for a good while and the glue will not be noticeable.

Selecting Carpet Fibers

Carpeting is available in a variety of fibers. Here are some facts worth remembering about the more common fibers:

1. *Nylon* is durable, colorfast, soil-resistant, cleans easily and wears well under heavy traffic.
2. *Polyester* has low static buildup, is soft, easily cleaned and takes heavy traffic.
3. *Wool* is warm, soil-resistant, easily cleaned, supports heavy traffic and is usually the most expensive.
4. *Acrylic* which is harder to clean, is light in weight, fluffy, feels more like wool and can stand heavy use.
5. *Olefin* is soil-resistant, durable, has low static buildup and is good for outdoors and bathrooms.
6. *Rayon* can stand only light use.

Quiet Carpeting

When buying carpeting consider its noise-absorbing qualities. Cut pile carpets absorb more noise than loop pile. The higher the pile, the more noise it absorbs. Backings also help to reduce noise. The more porous the backing, the more it reduces noise. If you have a choice, select cushions and backings of hair and jute because they absorb more noise than rubber and sponge.

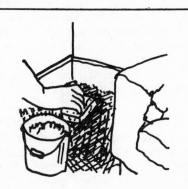

Cleaning Rugs and Carpets

When preparing to shampoo a rug or carpet, first vacuum thoroughly to remove as much surface dirt as possible, and then use one of many rug shampoos on the market. If you prefer, you can make your own rug shampoo. Mix ½ cup powdered detergent with two cups of warm water, and beat the mixture to a stiff foam. It should look like whipped cream. (An eggbeater can be used.) Beat the mixture again when the foam disappears.

It is important that when you shampoo the rug, the foam and *not* the water does the work. Apply with a sponge or long-handled sponge mop, using circular movements. Rinse well with a wet sponge until all the soap has been removed from the rug, and allow to dry.

One word of caution: It is recommended that you test an inconspicuous portion of your rug with the shampoo before doing the entire job.

Dusting Techniques

It is wise, when starting to dust, to begin at the top. Dust the higher areas and objects first. The dust that falls will land on the lower areas which you will be dusting later. Moisten the dusting cloth with the tiniest bit of furniture cleaner and the dust will stay on the cloth rather than the furniture.

To get at the dust and dirt in corners, cut an old whisk broom to a 45-degree angle, using a scissors or a razor blade. The tapered point will help you do a thorough job.

Floating Dust

To keep the dust from floating out, dampen the inside of your dustpan before sweeping dust into it.

Paper Stuck to Wood

Paper that has stuck to wooden surfaces will come off if a few drops of olive oil or peanut oil are allowed to soak into it. Rub paper off gently with a soft cloth. Do not use sharp object for removal.

Washing Woodwork

If painted woodwork has become discolored, clean it off with a solution made up of one gallon of water to which ¼ cup ammonia and two tablespoons of detergent have been added. Wash, then rinse with clear water.

Shellacking Baseboards

If you want to prevent dust from sticking to baseboards, apply a coating of shellac to the surface. Not only will the task of cleaning the corners be easier, but paint will not chip off as easily.

Window Sills

Window sills will be easier to clean if you protect them with a coating of floor wax. Wax prevents the dirt and rain from adhering and also protects the painted surface. When time for repainting arrives, make sure to remove the waxed surface.

Washing Walls and Ceilings

When washing a wall and ceiling in a room, wash the ceiling first. Rinse and dry the ceiling, and then follow the same procedure starting from the top of the wall and working downward. Working in this manner you will avoid dripping water and streaky surfaces.

Toothbrushes as Tools

Old toothbrushes are useful for cleaning those hard-to-get-at spots in the corner of windowpanes, baseboards, etc. The grout between tiles and around the bathtub can also be cleaned with a toothbrush. Also, use it on the kitchen sink and stove.

Cellar Dampness

Cellar dampness caused by condensation rather than direct leaks through the walls can be relieved by improving ventilation. An easy way to attack the problem is to keep an ordinary fan running in your basement. It should be positioned so that the stream of air is directed toward the cellar window which must be kept partially open.

Testing for Cellar Dampness

There are two tests to determine whether cellar dampness is caused by condensation. One test is to attach a small mirror to one of the walls with adhesive tape. In eight hours or less tiny drops of water will gather on the mirror if condensation is causing the dampness. The other test is to lay a rubber mat on the bare concrete floor and to remove it 24 hours later. If the floor is damp, it indicates that moisture has penetrated the concrete from below.

Cellar Walls and Floors

A special cellar waterproofing paint is available at paint stores that will solve many of your dampness and moisture problems. Check with your local dealer.

Venetian Blind Mittens

An old cotton mitten or glove will make the job of cleaning venetian blinds a lot easier. You can make your own mitten out of old towels by simply tracing the outline of your hand with a marking pencil. Make the tracing one inch larger than your hand. Lay this piece of toweling on a second piece, and cut both pieces at one time. Sew together, leaving one end open to receive your hand. Turn the sewn mitten inside out and you are ready to attack the blinds.

Window Washing

So often, it is difficult to tell whether the spot on your window that your polishing cloth didn't get is on the inside or the outside. One way of knowing for sure is to always polish the inside of the window with a sideways motion and the outside with an up and down stroke.

If you want your windows to shine, add a tablespoon or two of vinegar or ammonia to your wash-water.

Part Two

The Bathroom

▰▰▰▰▰▰▰▰▰▰▰▰▰▰▰▰▰▰▰▰▰▰▰▰▰

Toothbrush Conditioning

Before using a new toothbrush for the first time, soak it in cold water for 24 hours to strengthen the bristles.

Toothpaste Tubes

If your toothpaste tube springs a leak, clean and dry the spot where the toothpaste has oozed through the tube. Then, wrap the area with several turns of adhesive tape.

Other Uses of Toothpaste

Diamonds and other precious stones can be kept bright and sparkling by brushing them with toothpaste. After brushing for a few minutes, rinse in cold water.

For a thorough cleaning, soak diamonds in hot, sudsy water to which a few drops of ammonia has been added.

Skin Softeners

Government analyses show that the face creams of various com-panies are basically similar in chemical composition, and that vegetable oil can be just as effective in keeping the skin soft as the most expensive face cream. To help you make an informed purchase without wasting money, the FDA has a free reprint available from its magazine, the *FDA Consumer*. For your free copy of "Cosmetics—the Substances Beneath the Form," just send a postcard to the Consumer Information Center, Dept. 684E, Pueblo, Colorado 81009.

Sponges as Soap Dishes

Sponges which are no longer useful for wiping surfaces can be of service as soap-savers. A bar of soap placed on a sponge won't get soft and gooey on the bottom as it does in a soap dish, making a mess and wasting soap. Place the sponge in the soap dish. When the sponge becomes saturated with soap drippings, use it for cleaning up around sinks and wash basins.

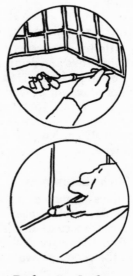

white tile cement with water. Keep the mixture loose so it will go on easily.

If this process fails to clean the joints properly, a mixture of muriatic acid and water will usually remove the remaining stains. Your hardware dealer can supply the acid.

Shower Curtains

Shower curtains often billow away from the side of the tub when warm air currents generated by hot water get under them. Curtains can be kept firmly in place by sealing small magnets in the bottom hem. The magnets will be attracted to the cast iron or steel under the porcelain of the bathtub.

Sweet Showers

Add ½ cup of chlorine bleach to a cup of warm water. Pour the solution into a spray bottle. Dry off the shower walls, then spray the shower tile walls with the chlorine solution. When completely covered wash the walls down with an old towel or with a sponge mop wrapped in toweling material. Repeat once each month to keep your shower mildew-free and sweet-smelling.

Bathroom Tile Joints

The mortar that joins the tiles in your bathroom usually darkens with age. You can postpone the darkening process by giving the joints a good scrubbing with a stiff brush. Follow this by by covering the areas that remain soiled with a paste that can be made by mixing

Bathroom Sealants

Silicone sealants developed and used in numerous aerospace applications are now available at all hardware stores in tubes, and are excellent products to fill in cracks and to fill in the space where your bathtub meets the tile floor and tile wall. In preparing the area, remove all the loose grout, and clean the area thoroughly. Then, press the grout out through the tube nozzle that is provided and run the sealant around the edge of the tub against the tiles. Wet your finger and smooth the grout to get neat results. Wash your hands immediately with soap and water.

Chipped Porcelain

An enamel made specifically for covering chipped porcelain in sinks and bathtubs is available at hardware stores. After the application, the area covered may be noticeable. Nevertheless, it will still look better than if it were not patched at all, and it will prevent spread of the deterioration.

Sweating Commodes

Those little beads of water that form on toilet tanks and drip on the floor can be avaided. A standard coat of floor wax will prevent the condensation from forming in many cases. Apply the wax at two-month intervals and your problem may be solved.

Silent Bathrooms

Silent valves are now available to replace the older style rubber bulbs which often produce loud flushing sounds. Your hardware dealer can show you the products available.

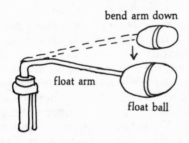

bend arm down

float arm

float ball

Toilet Tanks I

If your toilet tank runs constantly, the float arm in the tank may not be closing the water valve and may need adjustment. Try bending it down slightly. This will probably stop the flow of water.

Toilet Tanks II

A common cause of constantly running water in a toilet tank is a defective flush ball—the rubber or plastic ball that comes up when you press the outside flush lever down. This permits the water in the tank to flow into the bowl and to flush it.

To check the flush ball for proper operation, take off the top of the tank and flush the toilet. If the ball fails to drop down and completely cover the opening below it, the

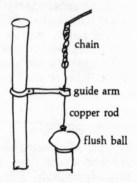

chain

guide arm

copper rod

flush ball

guide arm is slightly out of place. If so, move the arm until the ball drops down properly. If this does not solve the problem, press down on the rubber ball with your fingers. If this stops the noise of running water, the ball is worn out and needs to be replaced.

Clogged Toilet I

To clear a clogged toilet, use a toilet bowl plunger—a rubber cup with a curved skirt that fits *into* the throat of the bowl. Be sure there is enough water in the bowl to cover the rubber cup (to the point where it joins the wooden handle). Force the cup down and up with vigorous

toilet
bowl
plunger

motions until the clogged section appears to be free. Try again if the clogged material has not been dislodged. If the process does not work you will have to resort to a snake.

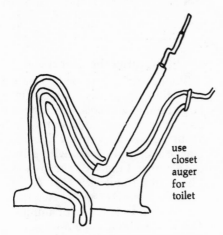

use
closet
auger
for
toilet

Clogged Toilet II

Clogged toilets that cannot be cleared by the ordinary use of a plunger can usually be cleared with a snake. The snake must be forced up the curve through which the water drains. Getting around the top of the curve and down the other side isn't easy, but it can be accomplished by pushing hard and turning the handle at the same time. When you buy a snake, get the type

known as a closet auger. It works better than other types that are on the market.

Cleaning the Toilet

Although there are bathroom brushes of various shapes and sizes on the market, it is best to choose one with the bristles set at a 45-degree angle to the handle (see illustration). This type of brush makes it easier to clean the area beneath the toilet bowl rim.

Toilet cleaner and liquid bleach should never be used at the same time, as the two together may combine to emit poisonous fumes. When using bathroom cleansers containing harmful chemicals, make sure the room is adequately ventilated.

Mounting Fixtures

It's easy to mount bathroom fixtures (soap dishes, etc.) with a number of the new cements made specifically for this purpose. The old practice of removing a tile in order to affix the fixture to the wall is no longer necessary. Your hardware dealer can suggest the proper adhesive.

Mildew Prevention

A piece of charcoal placed in a cup, and left in the corner of a room where mildew has a tendency to gather, will usually serve as an effective preventative.

Mildew on Bathroom Ceilings

If mildew is marring your bathroom ceiling, a good scrubbing with a strong solution of chlorine bleach will produce good results. If the ceiling is seriously mildewed, you may need to buy a small amount of trisodium phosphate (also called Beetsall) at a paint or hardware store, and add it to the bleach solution. To avoid having to repeat the process in a year or two, it may be wise to repaint the ceiling after you have cleaned it.

Hot Water Bags

To mend a rubber hot-water bag that has sprung a leak, dry it off thoroughly, and apply a piece of adhesive tape over the spot where it is leaking and it will hold temporarily. For permanent repair, apply an inner-tube patch. Kits of inner-tube patching materials can be purchased at automotive supply stores or bicycle shops.

Bathing Pets

When bathing dogs and cats, place steel wool in the drain opening to catch hairs and prevent clogging of the drain.

Cleaning the Bathtub

Since a bathtub must be cleaned each time it is used, which (in a large family) can be several times a day, it is a good idea not to use scouring powder repeatedly. Use a plastic sponge instead, with a mild detergent. This will remove the film left around the tub. A mild scouring powder can be used occasionally, and a solution of ammonia and water about once a week.

Chapter Four

CLEANING, REPAIRING AND PRESERVING HOUSEHOLD FURNISHINGS

Part One

Household Furniture and Accessories

●━━━━━━━━━━━━━━━━━━━━━━━

Home-made Furniture Restorer

If your furniture lacks luster, and has a dirty, dull finish which is an eyesore, one of the ready-made finishes available in hardware and paint stores may rectify the situation. If you have no luck with the standard products available, make your own. Here is a "recipe" which will provide you with a sufficient amount for testing:

4 tablespoons turpentine
4 tablespoons linseed oil

4 tablespoons white vinegar
1 tablespoon denatured alcohol.

Rub on to a small testing area, and polish with a soft cloth. If it works, make a larger amount by increasing the ingredients proportionately. Whatever is left over can be safely stored in a glass jar for future use.

Furniture Polisher

For polishing pieces of furniture with sharp corners and fancy molding, use a clean shoe buffer. The soft pad can reach the uneven spaces that are usually hard to get to.

White-ring Stains

Those unsightly white rings need not mar the surfaces of your table-tops permanently. Rub the area lightly with a chemically pure petroleum (like vaseline) and let it soak in overnight. Remove in the morning with a clean cloth. The mark will at least be lighter and may have disappeared altogether.

Shoe Polish as Stain

If you want to darken a scratched furniture surface, select a shoe polish of the same approximate color and buff the area.

Spots and Rings

Many spots or rings can be removed by rubbing the spot with a piece of soft cotton dampened with spirits of camphor, or with a solution of one part ammonia (or turpentine) mixed with one part linseed oil.

Black spots, usually caused by water penetrating a polished surface, cannot be removed superficially. You might try to remove the finish with steel wool soaked in methylated spirits, and follow this by bleaching the spot. Refinish with appropriate colored stain and varnish.

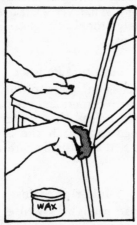

Cleaning Metal Furniture

After washing metal furniture with detergent and water, rinse and dry with a soft cloth. If the finish appears dull, polish with a white cream wax, the type made for kitchen appliances.

Protecting Your Mattress

To keep your mattress as sweet smelling as possible, do not place your bedsheet directly on the mattress. First cover the mattress surface with a mattress pad or with an old, clean sheet.

Adding Life to a Mattress

Keep a mattress from wearing unevenly by turning it over regularly. Turn an innerspring mattress once a month. Turn a mattress without springs once a week. The mattress will stay in better shape and you will always enjoy a good night's rest.

The Springs in Mattresses

Spray liquid wax directly on bedsprings to take the squeak out of them. Also, avoid rolling up innerspring mattresses, because you only weaken them by such repeated action.

Preserving Leather Furniture

Before soil has a chance to work its way into leather furniture, clean it with saddle or castile soap. Work up a good lather, and then remove it with a damp cloth. Follow this by wiping the leather dry.

Also, you might want to try one of the specially manufactured leather dressings available. It will help keep the leather pliable and prevent it from cracking. Your sports store or a department store stocks a variety of preparations.

Cleaning Leather Furniture

A quick, usually effective way of cleaning leather furniture is to dip a sponge in water to which the juice of half a lemon has been added.

Preventing Mildew on Wicker

To prevent mildew on hampers and baskets made of straw or wicker, coat the surface with two coats of shellac.

Sagging Cane Chairs

To take the sag out of the seat of a chair made of cane, wipe the surface with a cloth that has been dipped in hot water and wrung out. Scrub thoroughly, and then place chair outdoors in the sun to dry.

Loose Rungs

Chair rungs that have become loose, resulting in wobbly legs, can be easily fixed if glue is forced into the joints where leg meets rung, and the legs of the chairs are tied with rope until glue has hardened.

Cleaning Upholstery

To clean upholstery, first vacuum to remove as much loose dirt as possible, and shampoo with a mixture of ¼ cup powdered detergent and one cup warm water.

Whip the detergent into a foamy lather and apply it to small areas of the furniture at one time. When moving on to the next area, be sure to go back over the edges of the area you have just washed so overlapping areas will not appear when the upholstery has dried. After shampooing, wipe the area several times with a damp sponge to remove all traces of soap. Take an extra moment to dry off with a clean soft cloth to hasten drying.

Stained Brickwork

Whether the brickwork is indoors or outdoors, stains need never mar its surface permanently. Clean brick or stonework first with regular household detergent and warm water, and then allow to dry. When thoroughly dry, apply a thin coat of wood sealer and turpentine, mixed in equal parts.

Smoke-stained Bricks

If the brickwork around your fireplace has been tarnished by smoke stains, you can usually correct the situation with powdered kitchen cleanser and a good scrub. Occasionally that will not work effectively, in which case you should prepare a stiff paste made of talc mixed with trichloroethylene (available in hardware and paint stores) to spread over the stains. In order to retard the paste from drying rapidly, tape a piece of plastic over the area, and secure the edges with masking tape. After the paste beneath the plastic has dried, remove the covering and scrape, sand, or brush off the paste. The stains should be totally gone.

Cleaning a Fireplace

To clean a brick fireplace that doesn't have glaring stains, scrub it down with Beatsall (available in hardware stores) and hot water. Use two tablespoons per gallon. After using the Beatsall-water solution, rinse with clear water. When undertaking this job, wear rubber gloves and use an old terry towel or something similar for scrubbing.

Fireplace Logs I

Never store fireplace logs in your house. If you do, you may find that insects that have made their homes in the logs will eventually find their way into your furniture and into your carpeting. Bring into the house only as much wood as you will use in one day.

Fireplace Logs II

Do not use logs cut from soft wood such as pine, fir and cedar. These burn quickly and send off many sparks. Birch also burns quickly. Hardwood burns well, so try to purchase oak, walnut and fruitwood logs. They are sometimes more costly, but well worth the higher price.

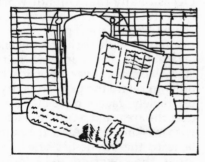

Home-made Logs

Ecology and thrift-minded individuals who use a fireplace will be interested in learning that "logs" can be made out of old newspapers and magazines. You can buy a portable logger, or you can roll your own. For more information about the ready-made unit, write to Logger Industries, 200 N. Stonestreet Avenue, Rockville, Maryland 20850.

Protecting Marble Surfaces

Marble table- and counter-tops are quite likely to become stained from spilled liquids and food. You can protect the surfaces by applying hard, automobile-type paste wax and polish to a shine.

Plastic Table-Tops

Plastic table-tops can be treated for stain removal in the same manner as marble surfaces. In addition, a protective coat can be added by rubbing ordinary toothpaste into the surface.

Shrinking Drapes

The more loose the weave of the fabric, the more likely it is that the material will shrink when washed. When buying draperies, look for those with hems that have extra material which can be pressed out in case of shrinkage. Also, try to purchase drapes that are even longer than the size you actually need, so that if they do shrink it will not be noticed. Of course, it is best to buy material that is *guaranteed* not to shrink.

Shining Mirrors

Tissue paper, crumpled up, can be used for shining newly washed windows or mirrors.

Cloudy Mirrors

To keep mirrors from becoming cloudy, position them in your home in spots where the sun will not shine directly on them.

Mirror Backs

Place a smooth piece of tinfoil over the bare spots that have developed on the back of a mirror. Secure the tinfoil in place with a coat of shellac.

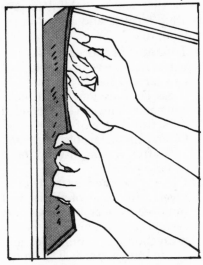

Cleaning Framed Mirrors

In order to prevent water from getting inside a mirror frame when you are cleaning it, hold a piece of cardboard against the inside edge of the mirror.

Stained Decanters

Stains that have developed in glass vases and decanters can be removed by soaking them in hot water containing a bit of vinegar. Areas smudged by grease can be cleaned with ginger ale or a cola soda drink.

Cleaning Bottles

Carpet tacks can be used to remove the sediment that has gathered on the bottom of a glass bottle or vase. Toss a handful of tacks into the warm, sudsy water in the bottle or vase. Give it a good shaking. The tacks will loosen the sediment.

Nicked Glassware

You can round off the sharp edges of nicked glassware by using "OO" sandpaper. Wrap the paper around the handle of a pencil and rub the paper across the nicked area until the sharp edges have disappeared.

Cleaning Plaster Ornaments

Dip the plaster ornaments you would like to clean in thick liquid starch, and then let them dry. Brush off the dry starch and you will find new luster added to your decorative pieces.

Cleaning Ashtrays

Ashtrays should be cleaned extra well from time to time to remove the clinging foul ordor that does not always disappear with normal washing. You can accomplish this by soaking the ashtrays in denatured alcohol diluted with water. One cup of alcohol to one cup of water will make up an effective solution.

Drip-free Candles

Keep your candles in the refrigerator for several hours before using them and they will drip less, and possibly not at all.

Smoking Candles

Candles will smoke less if the wicks are trimmed with scissors before use. Long wicks tend to smoke. Cut the wicks straight across so that the flame and candle burn evenly. Remove pieces of wick, match-sticks and other foreign particles from the cupped part of the candle, because they are the source of much of the smoking problem.

Wilting Candles

Candles have a tendency to wilt in hot weather. You can prevent this by dipping them in shellac that has been thinned with turpentine. Hang candles by the wicks, and allow them to dry. The shellac will stiffen the candle but not interfere with its burning. Three-pound cut shellac is best.

Candle Power

Candles set aside for blackouts and other emergencies should be at least ¾ of an inch thick and six or seven inches high. Be prepared with a glass chimney. Uncovered candles tend to flicker in the lightest draft and are a fire hazard, while a candle inside a glass chimney provides a warm steady light, burns slowly, and can be carried around without flickering or going out.

Decorative Candles

Decorative candles that have lost their luster can be enlivened by rubbing them with a soft cloth dampened in denatured alcohol.

Cleaning and Preserving Brass

There are a variety of suggested methods of restoring tarnished brass to its original luster. Here are some that will be helpful in preventing tarnish, and others in removing it.

1. To clean discolored brass, rub with a rag soaked in a mixture of vinegar and salt.
2. Brass doorknockers, doorknobs and nameplates can be protected by a thin layer of paste wax. Clean with metal polish first and buff after waxing. Rewax once or twice yearly.
3. Clean, polished brass that is given a thin coat of shellac will not need to be polished again. A second coat will give still better protection. The only cleaning needed thereafter will be an occasional dusting.
4. To clean tarnished brass, use a product such as Mr. Clean. Place cleaning agent in a plastic pail, add water, and a piece of aluminum foil. Leave the brass object in the solution for fifteen minutes. Rinse, then dry and polish.
5. Alternate method: Dip a lemon peel in salt and rub it on the brass object.

Brass Polish "Recipe"

To make your own brass polish, start with a cup of vinegar, add two tablespoons of salt and enough flour to make a smooth paste. Apply the paste to brass with a damp cloth to remove stains. Rub hard, rinse in cold water, and dry surface with a soft cloth.

Copper Cleaner

Salt and lemon juice or salt and vinegar is all it takes to clean copper. That and a good rubbing.

Copper Spot

Green spots, known as patina, will form on copper with the passage of time. To clean, saturate your cleaning cloth with a mixture of equal parts of water and ammonia. Dry off promptly and polish surface with a brass wax.

Quick Patina

To obtain the greenish effect on copper (and bronze) which normally occurs only after years of exposure to air, you can rub buttermilk on the object. Parts of it will turn green.

Cleaning Pewter

To clean articles made of pewter, use only hot, sudsy water. Rinse, dry off, and then apply a coating of silver polish.

Cleaning Cloths

Save your worn-out clothing. Coarse materials, including worn-out towels, are good for heavy cleaning; smoother ones for polishing. Also, there is no need to throw away old socks just because there are holes in the heels or toes. Cut off the tops and use them. They are ideal for use as soft polishing cloths.

Garbage Cans

Garbage cans will last longer and be easier to clean if the bottoms are coated on the inside with asphalt paint. Wash the inside of the can first. Pour a cupful of paint into the can and roll it around until the seams and crevices are covered. Make sure the coating reaches several inches up the sides of the can.

Sticky Wastebaskets

Coat the bottom of your wastebaskets with a polishing wax and continue the waxing up the sides. This will not only prevent damp and sticky objects from adhering to it, but will prevent the container from rusting.

Basic Household Cleaning
Tools and Products

Aside from their obvious uses, the following basic household items can be used successfully as cleaning tools and agents:

Baking Soda
Can be used to clean glass, wall tile, and porcelain enamel. An open box in the refrigerator will keep it odor-free.

Ammonia
Useful in cleaning ovens, loosening wax, and washing windows and mirrors.

Vinegar and Lemon Juice
Both products are useful agents in removing hard-water spots. They are also helpful in removing rust stains from sinks.

Bleach
Can be helpful in removing some stains, but test it first. It can mar the shiny finish of sinks, bathtubs, and kitchen appliances. Use with caution.

Steel Wool and Soap Pads
Especially useful on aluminum articles, these products can help remove hard-to-get-off foods from pots, pans, and oven racks.

Brooms
Fiber brooms are more expensive, but they last longer. Brooms, when not in use, should be hung up or should rest on their handles (and not on the fibers).

Dustpans
Dustpans with long handles are most useful. You will be saved the effort of bending to pick up the dirt.

Dry Mops and Dust Mops
Use mops with removable heads. These can be washed and dried more easily.

Sponge and String Mop
Like the dry mop, the sponge and string mop should have a removable head. When making your purchase, be sure the handle is long enough to be comfortable for your height.

Vacuum Cleaners
Lightweight vacuums are best for use on wood floors. The canister (tank) type is a good all-purpose cleaner. If the vacuum is to be used mainly on rugs and carpets, the upright is the preferred type.

Pails
Having two pails, one for washing and one for rinsing, will make your work easier. Be sure the size is right to accommodate your mops.

Reaching Aids
Every household needs a sturdy stool or a short stepladder (about three feet high) to reach the hard-to-get-at spots. Aluminum ladders are easiest to handle because of their light weight.

Part Two

Care of Hobby and Sports Equipment

━━━━━━━━━━━━━━━━━━━━━━━━━━

Cassette Tapes

If the tape pulls out of your cassette or 8-track cartridge, and if it is still not crinkled or stretched, turn the cartridge upside down and allow tape to dangle. Then, jerk the tape as you would a window shade. The tape will wind back up like a shade on spring rollers.

Piano Care

Temperatures exceeding high or low will hurt a piano. Keep the instrument away from windows that are opened in the winter, and away from radiators and steampipes. The piano will stay in tune longer.

A piano must be used periodically to stay in good condition. It should be played once a week, or at least the keys should be exercised, even if it's only through the act of dusting them.

Piano Keys

For your piano keys to retain their whiteness, avoid keeping them covered constantly. Keys will stay white longer if exposed to the light of day, particularly sunlight.

Piano Key Cleaning

White piano keys will retain their whiteness if you clean them with milk or yogurt. Make sure no liquid seeps into the cracks between the keys. Markings on the keys caused by marking pens and pencils can usually be removed by using a laundry detergent.

Adding Life to Batteries and Film

Photographic film and batteries have a limited shelf-life. The expiration date is marked on all film. You can greatly prolong the life of both film and batteries if you will wrap them tightly in waterproof plastic sheets or bags, and then secure the package with tape or rubber bands. Then, store the protected package on the bottom shelf of your refrigerator until needed.

Film Processing

A simple way of keeping the developing solution moving while prints are being developed is to put a pencil or a length of dowel under the developing tray. Now, the tray can be moved to and fro more easily without worrying about splashing.

Golf Clubs Care

A simple way of keeping new golf clubs looking good is to rub them with clear shoe polish wax. This will preserve their shine and prevent early rust and corrosion.

Fishing Sinkers

If you like to fish, you would be well advised not to discard the old nuts, bolts and large washers that you come across from time to time. Save them, and use them as sinkers when you go fishing next time.

Warping Records I

To prevent records from warping, it is important that you remove the wrappers from the covers as soon as possible. When wrappers heat up, they contract and often warp the records.

Warping Records II

A warped record can be straightened out. Place the record between two pieces of glass large enough to cover the full diameter. Allow to sit in the sun for two or three hours, and the record will resume its original shape.

Chapter Five

TOOLS
AND
PROCEDURES
FOR
INTERIOR
PROJECTS

Part One

The Care and Use
of Basic Tools

Hammering Nails

Every home should have at least one good hammer for general purposes. A hammer weighing from 12-16 ounces will serve most requirements. A 16-ounce hammer is most commonly used. For more hitting power, hold the hammer near

the end of the handle. When starting the nail, hold it firmly and tap it gently into the wood until it takes hold—then drive it in.

Types of Hammers

The ordinary claw hammer (also called a nail hammer) is specifically designed for nails. Its face, the part that strikes the nail head, is tempered for soft steel nails. When used on hardened steel such as cold chisels, or even on the hardened nails used in concrete work, the face of a claw hammer may chip,

and fragments of steel may fly into the worker's eyes. Use a ball hammer, or a hand-drilling hammer to strike hardened steel nails, cold chisels, and star drills.

Hammering a Chisel

Hammering on a cold chisel or star drill can produce an uncomfortable stinging sensation. If wearing gloves or wrapping a sponge around the chisel doesn't offer enough protection, make a protective handle for the chisel out of a small hollow rubber ball. Cut a hole in the ball the same diameter

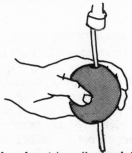

as the chisel handle, and force the handle through the ball. By squeezing the ball you'll be able to grip the tool tightly and hammer without the unpleasant sting.

Nailing Hardwood

If you are having trouble having your nails penetrate hardwood, dip them in oil or apply soap to them to facilitate entry.

Cabinet Nailing

When you are making a cabinet or doing some other type of work where you do not want the wood to be marred, do not drive the nail all the way into the wood. Allow it to protrude about ⅛ of an inch and use a nail-set (or another nail) to drive it in the balance of the way.

Removing Nails I

There is an easy way to remove a nail from a piece of wood, as long as the head is somewhat above the surface. Grasp the head of the nail with the claw hammer, slide a block of wood under the head of the hammer, and push the hammer back against the block. If the nail is long, use a thicker piece of wood. The nail will come out with little effort and may even be straight enough to be re-used.

Prevent Wood-splitting

If nails (instead of glue) are used to join two pieces of wood, the wood will often split, especially if the nails are driven into the wood very close to the edge. The problem is easily solved by either drilling a small pilot hole before nailing, or by cutting (or blunting) the point of the nail before hammering it in. Another method that usually works well is to drive the nail in at an angle.

Removing Nails II

Stubborn nails under which you cannot fit your claw hammer can usually be brought up by using a pair of cutting pliers. When the nail head is about ⅛- or ¼-inch above the wood, insert your claw hammer and extract the nail in the usual manner.

Removing Nails III

If you want to save a piece of wood for future use and a nail is protruding that you cannot extract with your claw hammer, cut off the head of the nail as close to the wood as possible with a hacksaw or cutting pliers. Then, hammer nail into wood with a nail-set and cover hole with wood filler. If the point of the nail comes out at the other end, extract with a pair of cutting pliers and fill the opening with filler.

Popping Nails

The seasonal contraction and expansion of house studs often pushes out the nails that are holding the plasterboard until they protrude through the wallpaper or painted surface. Pull out protruding nails, if possible, and fill the nail holes with plaster. Otherwise, drive in ring-

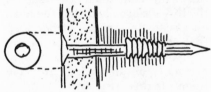

shank nails an inch above or below the nails that have popped. Ring-shank nails have extra holding power and will not pop.

Concealing Nails

Aside from the normal way of concealing nails (driving them below the surface of the wood with a nail-set and then filling the indentation with wood filler), an effective way of hiding nails is to prepare a cover for them. This is done by pushing a wood chisel into the surface of the wood to a depth of about 1/16 or 1/8 of an inch, and then

pushing the chisel on a plane parallel with the wood to make a tongue about one inch long. The tongue will curl up, and you will be able to drive a finishing nail into the space. Recess the nail with a nail-set, and then smear glue over the area. Press down and apply a weight. When the glue has bonded the two surfaces sand off excess glue.

Removing Headless Nails

If the nail you are trying to remove has lost its head, grip it with a pair of pliers. Then, while holding the pliers with one hand, use a claw hammer to raise both the pliers and the headless nail.

Temporary Nailing

Temporary wooden structures that have been nailed together can be more easily dismantled when duplex head nails are used. These nails have two heads, one at the

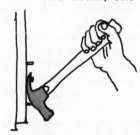

very end, and the other about an inch below (see illustration). When driven into wood, the nail stops at the lower head, leaving the upper head protruding so it can be removed by a claw hammer.

The Staple Gun

Staple guns are tremendous time-savers and are dependable for heavy and light work. They take staples from ¼-inch to ½-inch and will penetrate the hardest woods without too much effort. The staple gun has dozens of practical uses, from holding glued parts in place until they dry, to making or repairing screens, and installing ceiling tiles.

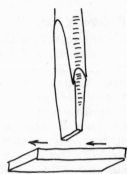

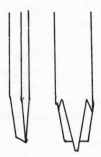

Screwdriving

Each household should have two types of screwdrivers: the straight blade and the Phillips. Both come in a variety of sizes. Always push against the head of the screw when you turn both the standard single-slot screwdriver and the Phillips. Should you find yourself having to insert or remove a Phillips head screw, and not having a Phillips screwdriver, a straight blade will do the trick as long as it fits snugly into the groove and will not keep coming out of the groove as you work.

Caring for Screwdrivers

The important thing to know about the care of screwdrivers is that the edge (the blade tip) must be squared occasionally so that pointed or rounded edges do not form. Use a file to keep blade-tip flat and square, or grind it down with a coarse oil stone or electric grinder. If your screwdriver blade is in proper condition it will fit snugly into the screw slot and will not slip.

Screws in Hardwood

Driving screws into hardwood can be difficult, and a little soap on the threads usually makes the job a lot easier. Save pieces of bar soap that are too small for use in the bath or shower (and that would normally be discarded) and use them for this purpose.

Hiding Screw Heads

Screw heads can be concealed by the use of round, wooden plugs. For a medium-size screw, drill a ½-inch hole ¼-inch deep. Drill a second hole in the middle of the first one with a bit slightly narrower than the thickness of the screw shank. Turn the screw into the second hole until its head is flush with the bottom of the ½-inch hole.

Make a plug by cutting off a ¼-inch slice of a ½-inch wooden rod or dowel. Place a little glue on the underside of the plug and slip it into the hole. The plug may be sanded flush with the surface, or you may allow it to protrude for decorative effect.

Enlarged Screw Holes

Hinges and handles become ineffective and difficult to use when the screw hole has become enlarged. To correct the situation, first make sure that the wood surrounding

the hinge or handle is not split. If it is, remove the hinge or handle, fill the split with a wood filler and let it dry. Also, make a tapered wood-plug (or use wooden match sticks), and force it into the opening. Make a pilot hole with your drill or with an awl, and then insert the screw.

Small Parts Storage

A good way to store nails, screws, nuts, bolts, and other small parts which you will be using often is in glass jars that once contained baby food, apple sauce, or mustard. Any kind of jar with a screw-on cap will do the job. Simply pierce a hole in the center of the metal lid with a drill or a nail, place the lid in position beneath a shelf and screw it into place. Use a washer under the screw to prevent the lid from turning when unscrewing the jar.

Using Old Gloves

Don't throw your old gloves away. If they are still in reasonably good condition, nail them within easy reach of your bench and you can use the glove fingers for nail-punches, small screwdrivers and other small tools that you find yourself reaching for regularly.

Preserving Washers and Nuts

Washers and nuts are easily lost. A good way to keep them from being lost or misplaced is to slip them over the open end of a large safety or diaper pin. Close the pin and suspend it from a nail or store it in a container.

Stubborn Nuts I

A nut that is badly rusted can sometimes be removed by repeated application of a penetrating oil such as Liquid Wrench. Pour the oil, a few drops at a time, into the crack around the edges of the bolt. Allow the oil to sink in. After the second application give the bolt several sharp blows with a hammer. Repeat this procedure several times until the nut loosens.

If this doesn't work, build a wall of putty around the frozen nut. Pour a little penetrating oil into the area inside the wall. Wait for several hours, remove the oil and putty and turn the nut. If the nut is not freed after the first application, give it one more try with the penetrating oil.

Stubborn Nuts II

One way to remove a nut which has resisted your efforts with a wrench is to heat it with a propane torch. Best results will be obtained if you adjust the torch to produce a small cone of flame. Direct the flame only at the nut. As the nut warms up, the hardened rust or paint will become loose enough to allow the nut to be turned with a wrench.

Stubborn Nuts III

Specially designed nutcrackers are available at better hardware stores. All that is required to crack the stubborn nut is to continue applying pressure to it until it splits. The tool is costly, and is a must if the above two hints are not effective.

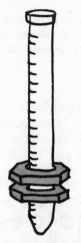

Slipping Nuts

To keep nuts from loosening, place a few drops of shellac on the bolt just before you give it the final, full turn. The shellac will hold the nut tight, but not so tight that you'll have difficulty loosening it later.

Another way to keep a nut from shifting is to add a second nut of the same size to the bolt. Tighten it against the first one and the second nut will keep the first securely in place.

Locating Studs

If you have tried other methods and failed, a good way to locate studs is to remove the molding at the bottom of the wall. There you will probably see where the sheets or plasterboard have been joined, which would indicate the location of a stud. If for some reason, it is still not clear, drive in nails every few inches along the area that was covered by the molding until your nail hits a stud. All marks and nail heads will be covered when you replace the molding. After you have located one stud, in a properly built house, the next stud will be 16 inches away—measuring from the center of one stud to the center of the next.

Washer Power

A washer placed beneath the head of a screw greatly adds to its holding power. The reason is that the washer enlarges the base of the screw so that it presses against a greater area.

Corrugated Fasteners

Corrugated fasteners are more effective than nails in holding small pieces of wood together. The divergent type in which the center corrugations diverge from each other are especially effective because they lock the two pieces together. Corrugated fasteners are also useful in holding together glued mitered pieces such as the corners of picture frames.

Rubber Grips for Pliers

For a more comfortable and a more secure grip, place a continuous piece of rubber hose over both handles of a pair of pliers. The rounded part of the hose will keep the pliers open when you relax your grip. The heavy rubber tubing will serve as a safety device by insulating the handles and preventing an electric shock when you are performing electrical work. The rubber hose will also make it easy to hang up your tool when it is not being used.

Adding Life to Sandpaper

To add longevity to sandpaper, apply a stiff backing down the center of the sandpaper with a strip of masking tape. This will keep the sandpaper from tearing or creasing, even when you are using a sanding block on a relatively

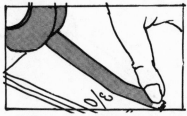

smooth surface. You'll get three times as much use from the sandpaper this way.

Picking Up Pins and Tacks

Picking pins and tacks up with a magnet does not always do the job well. A piece of paper placed over the magnet before picking up the pieces will make it easier to handle them once you've got them.

Handling Steel Wool

To keep the bits of steel from penetrating your skin when using steel wool, cut a hollow rubber ball

in half and place the pad in one of the halves. Bear down as hard as is necessary without worrying about picking up slivers. In addition, you'll find that the steel wool will last longer.

A Handy Shaver

The simple wood-shaver illustrated here is one of the handiest tools to have around the house. Its use calls for no talent or experience, and anyone can use it. Manufactured by the Stanley Tool Co., and called Surform, shaving down a door or drawer that has become too tight is a simple job that can be done quickly. The blades last a long time before becoming dull, and are replaceable.

Rust Prevention I

Tools rust when they absorb moisture from the air, and an easy way to prevent the damage is by placing moth balls or moth crystals in the tool box. You might also try to obtain little cloth bags of granules used to absorb moisture. Many hardware stores carry this product. When these granules are saturated with moisture, they change color. By putting them in the oven for a few minutes you will dry them out and they can be used again.

Rust Prevention II

Keep a few pieces of carpenter's blue chalk in your tool box and you will find that it will absorb moisture that would otherwise cause your tools to rust. From time to time warm the chalk in an oven to evaporate the moisture, and use the chalk again.

Disk Sharpeners

It requires more effort to cut with dull knives and tools. A variety of grinding tools and honing stones are available, but the old-fashioned disk sharpener is one of the least expensive and easiest to use. You can probably find one if

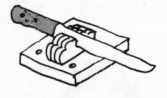

you check at your local hardware or variety store. Disk sharpeners can be kept or mounted on a wooden block or on your counter. Pass the blade to be sharpened through the disks, exerting maximum pressure as you bring the knife toward the body.

Wrapping Tools

When tools are not to be used for a long period, you can preserve them and protect them from rust by wrapping them in an oil-soaked rag. Of course, the oily rag may be a safety hazard, so it's best to store such tools in a metal box. Wrapping tools will also protect cutting edges from coming into contact with other tools that might chip or dull the sharp edges.

Lubricating Power Tools Regularly

Do make sure you lubricate power tools regularly, unless the manual instructs you not to. Keep track of the dates when they were last lubricated. Record dates on a central sheet tacked to the wall of your workshop or attach the date directly to each piece by writing it on masking tape.

Cleaning a File

Files will usually clog up and one good way of getting rid of embedded shavings and sawdust is to stretch a piece of adhesive tape over it. Place the tape on the file lengthwise, and press it down firmly. Pull the tape off sharply. Repeat with new tape, if necessary.

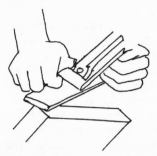

The Right Way to Use a Plane

A plane is used primarily for smoothing the edges of boards, and the best way to do this is to cut very fine shavings. Adjust the plane iron so that it barely protrudes below the bottom of the plane. Push the plane forward at a slight angle to the length of the board for easy cutting. Several fine cuts are better than one thick one.

Drawing a Straight Line

If you want to draw a straight line on a wall, you do not need to mark *two* points. Select the height at which you want the line drawn, and place your level at that point. When the bubble in the glass indicator is in the center, draw your line, and you can be certain it is straight.

Drawing a Long Straight Line

When you need to draw a long straight line, select the two points and drive nails into the surface. Tie a length of string to both nails and rub chalk on the string. Use blue chalk if the surface is white. Make sure the string is taut. Hold the string in the middle with the thumb and middle finger, pull out one or two inches and snap the string against the surface by releasing it. A straight chalk line will thus be laid down on the surface.

Reading a Ruler

When taking measurements, especially for cabinet work, it's important to be accurate. If you place a ruler or tape measure against the object to be measured and try to read it while looking at it from any angle other than a right angle, you will get a wrong reading. The proper way to take a reading is to lay the measuring tool flat and position yourself so you are looking directly over the spot where the end of the object being measured touches the ruler or tape.

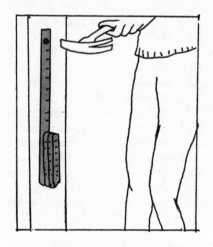

A Plumb Line Ruler

To check on whether a pole or a piece of furniture is absolutely vertical, drill a hole through the one-inch mark of your ruler. Tack the ruler to the top of the piece being straightened by driving a nail through the hole at the one-inch mark. The nail should be smaller than the hole. When the piece being straightened lines up with the ruler, you can be sure it's truly vertical.

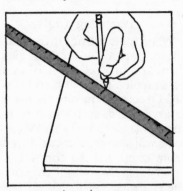

Dividing by Three

Dividing boards nine inches wide or less into three equal parts need not pose a mathematical problem. Lay the ruler *diagonally* across the board, with the one-inch mark at the corner of the board and the ten-inch mark at the edge. Make pencil marks on the board at the four-inch and the seven-inch marks on the tape. Use a T-square to draw straight lines through the marks. Regardless of the width of the board, the three sections will be equal.

Cutting Plasterboard

Plasterboard can be cut with a fine-toothed saw, but a better and easier method is to score and snap the material. Scoring should be done with a sharp utility knife, drawn along a straight edge. Cut through the paper on the side of the plasterboard that will be facing the room. Be sure to press down sufficiently hard to cut through the plaster. Place a piece of wood under the plasterboard sheet with the edge of the wood along the cut line, and snap off the overhanging piece of wood by pressing down on it. Cut through the paper backing on the reverse side to complete the job.

Measuring With a Tape

When you want to measure an article that would usually require assistance, you can manage it yourself. Use scotch tape or cloth tape to hold down one end of your steel or cloth measuring tape at your starting point. This will leave you free to move and stretch the tape as far as necessary without dislodging the other end from its set position.

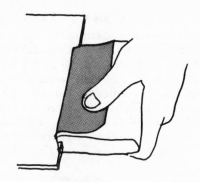

Sanding Flat Boards Without Their Slipping

A bit of preparation before proceeding will keep flat boards from slipping while being sanded. The idea is to place the board on a skid-free surface, and strips of foam rubber, such as a carpet cushion pad, will provide just such a surface. Foam rubber scraps are often available at no cost in stores that sell carpets. If not available to you, you can buy self-sticking weatherstripping in hardware stores. Either surface will prevent boards from slipping despite the vibrations caused by your electric sander.

Sanding Glass

To smooth the sharp edges of glass, fit a piece of sandpaper over the grooved end of a piece of wood flooring. Keep the sandpaper loose enough so you can fit the glass edge

into the sandpaper. Push back and forth with pressure applied. When the sandpaper is worn, shift the sandpaper on the block.

Drilling Holes in Bottles

Drilling a hole through the side of a glass bottle that you are planning to convert into a lamp can be very difficult with an ordinary twist-bit and electric drill. The bit won't bite into the glass and will tend to wander over the surface of the glass. If this happens use a spear-point carbide bit (not a masonry bit). Best results will be obtained if you use a variable speed electric drill that operates at very low speeds. Start your drilling at a low speed, and increase the RPMs as the hole begins to take shape. Lubricate the drill point with cool water from time to time as you are drilling, and do not press too hard.

Cutting Glass

Wax will hold a ruler or a straight-edge in place when cutting glass. Normally, these have a tendency to shift. Make a heavy mark on the glass with a wax crayon and place your wood or metal ruler over the wax.

Cutting Glass Containers

If you want to cut down the size of a jar, bottle, or other glass container, the best way is to fill the vessel with light oil (automobile oil will do) to the height you wish it to be cut. Then, heat a steel rod over a flame until it becomes red hot, holding the rod with pliers. A nail will do if you don't have a rod. Dip

the red hot rod into the oil and the glass will break evenly at the height of the oil. Remove sharp edges and burrs by rubbing with emery paper or by grinding with an abrasive wheel.

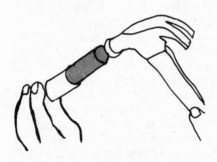

Cutting Metal Tubing

Before starting to cut through metal tubing, drive a short length of dowel into the tube. Then cut through both the tube and the dowel. The dowel will keep the teeth of the saw from catching against the edges of the tube with every stroke of the saw.

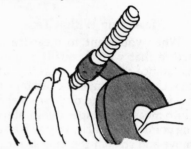

Cutting Metal Casing

There's a simple way to avoid sharp, ragged edges. When using a hacksaw to cut cable encased in metal, wrap the metal casing with friction tape at the cutting point, and cut through both tape and cable. The edges of the cable will end up smooth and slide more easily into the electrical boxes.

Keeping Track of Small Parts

When taking apart equipment and appliances, it is easy to lose screws, bolts, and washers. To prevent this, spread a strip of double-faced cellophane tape on the working table. The tape will stick to the table and the small parts will stick to the tape.

Soldering Wires

Before soldering electrical wires, twist them together in a firm mechanical joint. To solder properly, apply flux or use solder in wire form with a flux core and heat the wire joint with the tip of the soldering iron. In a few seconds the wires will be hot enough to melt the solder. Remove the soldering iron and touch the solder to the wires until the melted metal covers the joint. When the solder is fully melted, it will have turned to a shiny, silver finish.

An easier way to solder electrical wires is by applying steel solder. The bond is not as strong, but if wrapped well in tape, the bond will hold.

To Make Sawing Easier

Rub a bar of soap along either side of the blade of a saw and along the teeth. The blade will move through the wood with much greater ease. The soap will not stain the wood.

Keeping Saws Sharp

You can avoid the time and expense of getting your saws resharpened or having to replace blades, if you get into the habit of sawing properly. What's important is to exert pressure *only* when you are *pushing* the saw down through the wood—away from your body. When drawing the saw back, lift it away from the wood slightly so no pressure is exerted against the object being sawed. Your blades will remain sharper longer, and sawing will require less energy.

Saws that Bind

The cut, called the kerf, produced by a hand saw when cutting a board with the grain sometimes closes in on the blade and binds it. One way to avoid that binding is by pushing a nail or wedge of wood into the kerf at its open end. The insert will keep the kerf open until you finish sawing.

Sawing Sticky Wood

Sawing wood containing much resin creates a sticky problem. To prevent sticking, squirt denatured alcohol along the line of the cut. Because the alcohol evaporates quickly, spray only about 12 inches down the saw line at a time. When the alcohol evaporates, the wood will not be stained.

Hacksaw Blades

There are coarser blades and finer blades that can be used with hacksaws. Coarse blades cut faster and last longer. They should be used for most jobs. The smaller the surface being cut, the finer the blade that should be used. At least three teeth of the blade should engage the surface being cut. If with the blade you have selected only one or two of the teeth will be doing the cutting, choose a finer blade.

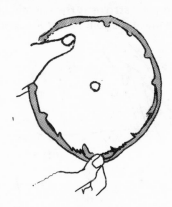

Protecting Circular Blades

Circular saw blades will stay sharp longer if protected when stored. An inch-wide cross-section of an old inner tube stretched around the blade of the saw will protect the teeth. Protect your fingers when putting the rubber around the blade by wearing gloves.

Sawing Correctly

When starting to cut into a board, it helps to brace the saw against your thumb. For safety's sake, do not brace the saw against the *tip* of your thumb. Bend your thumb and brace the saw against your knuckle. In that way you can start your cut on the pencil mark

rather than somewhere near it. Begin your stroke at the end of the blade and take long, slow strokes.

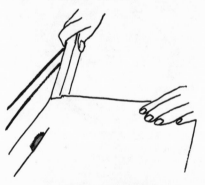

Table Saw Safety

Keep your hands at least six inches from the blade when operating a table saw, and stand to one side of the cutting line, so that if the piece being cut binds, and then flies back, it will not hit you. Above all, always use a push stick when pushing the wood through to make narrow cuts.

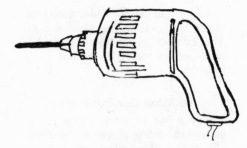

Homemade Bits

You can save on the cost of bits for electric drills by using nails for bits. Select a nail with the proper diameter for your job, and cut off the head of the nail with any metal cutter or hacksaw. Slide the nail into your drill as you would any bit. Tighten, and go to work!

Removing Molding

It is very easy to ruin your wall if you attempt to remove the molding and are not sufficiently careful. The best tool you can use for this purpose is a flat prybar. Insert the curved end behind the molding, preferably at a spot where there is a two-by-four behind the plaster. To be extra safe, place a large ¼-inch piece of plywood (at least 18 inches by 5 inches) against the wall before using the prybar. Pry up slowly until the molding is loose. Then, move to the next section until all the nails holding the molding have been loosened.

Power Tool Precautions

When working with power tools, particularly electric drills and saws, do not wear loose clothing that can get caught in the tool. If your hair is long, put it up in a bun or wear a cap. And, do not wear jewelry, even rings, that can interfere with the operation of the tool and cause accidents.

Magnetic Tool Rack

Magnetic knife racks are ideal for

frequently used hand tools. No hooks, holes or notches are needed to keep pliers, chisels and screw-drivers where they're easy to locate. Attached to the top of a ladder with screws or clamps, a magnetic rack provides easy access to tools that would otherwise have to be kept in the worker's belt. When purchasing a rack, test the unit to

make sure the magnets are powerful enough to hold the heavier tools.

Part Two

Simple Repair Procedures

━━━━━━━━━━━━━━━━━━━━━━━━━━━

Removing Dents From Metal

When removing dents from a metal object, if the dented area can be placed over a box of sand, you're in luck. Pound out the dents from the inside with a rubber mallet. If you do not have a mallet, convert a hammer into a mallet by putting a rubber tip over the face of the hammer. Use tips normally placed under chair and table legs. These are available at most hardware stores.

Dents in Wood

It is best to remove dents in wood as soon as possible. Pour hot water into the hollow area and allow to

stand. This will cause the compressed fibers to swell. If that fails, place a damp cotton cloth over the dented area and heat it with an electric iron. The moist heat will cause the wood to expand and raise the indentation. Allow the wood to dry thoroughly before rewaxing the area.

Filling Splits in Plywood

Whether the plywood is old or new, wood filler can be used to fill in split or cracked sections. Use burlap to rub the filler into the cracks, working across the grain. Sand the area when the filler has dried, and then paint.

Deep Gouges in Furniture

The best way to fill holes and deep gouges in a furniture surface is with a stick of solid shellac, available in the usual furniture colors. Soften one end of the stick by applying a lit match to it. Then, slice off pieces of the softened material with a knife or a flexible spatula.

Apply the softened shellac to the hole and smooth over with the blade. The repaired area can be covered with fresh varnish, lacquer, or the same material as was there originally.

Wood Filler

For filling cracks or small holes in wood, use a commercial wood filler or make your own by mixing fine sawdust with glue. Another type of wood filler can be made by mixing glue, tissue paper, linseed oil and chalk. If the mixture appears too light, add a dark tinting pigment which is available in paint stores. Apply the filling with a putty knife,

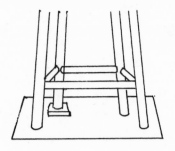

and after it dries, sand the area if necessary.

Wobbly Furniture

A wobble in a wooden chair or table may be caused by unevenness in one or two of the legs. Place the chair on a level surface to determine which legs are shorter. Push a piece of cardboard or wood under the short leg until it fits snugly. This will tell you how much needs to be cut from the other legs. Once the chair is steady, remove the wood or cardboard and use it to mark how much has to be cut. Use sandpaper to round off the cut edges.

Chapter Six

REPAIRING
AND
RESTORING
HOUSE
INTERIORS

Part One

Doors, Drawers, and Windows

Loose Drawer Knobs

When a dresser or cabinet knob is loose, tighten it by turning the knob clockwise. If the knob remains loose, simply open the drawer and insert a screwdriver into the slot on the head of the screw that holds the knob. Hold the screwdriver firmly with one hand and with the other tighten the knob. Sometimes the threads of the knob itself are worn out, in which case remove the knob and insert one or two short lengths of a flat toothpick, or any flat piece of wood or cardboard, into the hole of the knob. Then, while holding the screw with the screwdriver inside the drawer, replace and tighten the knob.

Loose Door Knobs I

Those old-fashioned door knobs that come loose in your hand are easily fixed. Put the loose knob back on the square, threaded shaft that holds both knobs together. Hold one knob and turn the other until both are tight. Tighten the set-screw at the base of each knob and

jiggle the knob as you tighten so the screw will stay in the groove.

If this doesn't work, the threads on either the shaft or the knob are probably worn, and you will have to replace the knob or the shafts. Your local hardware store should have the parts you require.

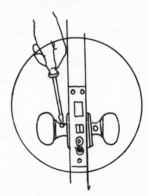

Loose Door Knobs II

Before purchasing new parts to replace a rattling door knob, try this procedure: Loosen the set-screw on the knob (see illustration). Remove the knob, put a small amount of putty or modeling clay in it, and then screw the knob back on.

Squeaky Doors

Aerosol spray cans of silicone lubricant are available in hardware stores. Sprayed on door hinges, the lubricant will stop doors from creaking.

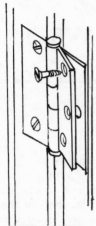

Sagging Doors

Old wooden doors have a tendency to sag because the screws in the hinges have worked loose. If the lower corner of the door touches the floor and the upper corner sticks to the frame, try tightening the screws of the upper hinge. If the door still sticks, put a thin piece of cardboard under the bottom hinge leaf on the door jamb and tighten its screws. Reverse the treatment if the lower corner sticks.

Sticking Doors

If tightening the hinge screws does not stop the door from sticking, you may have to remove the door and plane down the edge on the latch side. If it sticks only slightly, sandpapering with heavy-grit sandpaper may do the trick.

Sliding Doors

To keep sliding doors from sticking, dust the grooved track through which the door slides, and apply a thin coat of paste wax. Buff to a smooth finish.

Warped Doors

Moisture is the cause of warped doors, and removing the dampness will often rectify the warping. A heat lamp directed at the bulging side should dissipate the dampness. As soon as the warp disappears, remove the heat, and cover both sides and all edges of the door with sealer to prevent further absorption of moisture.

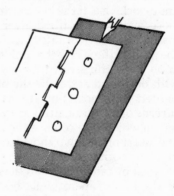

Doors That Won't Close

If your door tends to spring open, the problem is probably due to a hinge which is too deeply set. Remove the hinge, place a piece of cardboard under it, and trace its outline with a sharp pencil. Now, cut the cardboard, place it under the hinge and reset the screws. This will raise the hinge. If the hinge jams, it may be because the screws have not been tightened sufficiently.

Drafty Doors

If too much of a draft is coming in through the bottom of an outside door, you can correct the situation

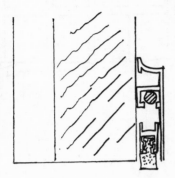

by attaching a simple device available in practically any hardware store: an aluminum frame with a movable strip of neoprene. The strip drops to the floor when the door is shut and lifts up when opened.

There is also available a less expensive frame in which a strip of plastic or rubber can be moved up and down manually. Either product will help conserve energy in the summertime and in the wintertime.

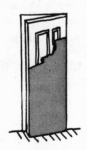

Modernizing Old Doors

Old doors can be modernized by simply gluing or nailing panels of plywood to the old surface. Plywood that is ¼-inch thick will do the job. When attaching the plywood with glue, remove the paint from the old door first so the glue will stick. After the paint has been removed, wash surface with alcohol.

For Easy-sliding Cabinet Doors

Cabinet doors that slide in ordinary grooves routed into the wooden frames (not using the special hardware that is available) can be made to move more smoothly by applying some shellac to the surface and then adding wax. Apply a thin coat of shellac to the inside of the groove and the bottom of the door. When dry apply ordinary polishing wax. Even a candle will do the trick.

Shallow Closets

Narrow clothes closets sometimes must remain without doors because there is no room for the door to swing. In such cases try attaching a full length bamboo blind. It is not only decorative, but will keep your clothes from full view while providing adequate ventilation.

Broken Window Pane

You may not have the time to replace a pane of glass the moment it cracks. If that is the case, paint over the crack on the inside of the window with fresh white shellac. The shellac will hold the glass together *temporarily*, and will keep out the wind and rain. Being clear, it will not interfere with your vision.

Removing a Broken Key

Work a thin jigsaw blade into the cylinder next to the broken key, and twist the blade and pull outward until you feel the teeth catching the key. Pull the blade out *slowly*, and you may succeed in bringing the key out. It may take more than one try to succeed.

Sticky Locks

When a key doesn't work easily, and the lock is difficult to turn, an aerosol can of silicone lubricant, which is available in hardware stores, will solve your problem. Spray the lubricant on the key and directly into the lock. Push key in and pull out several times so the lubricant saturates the keyhole.

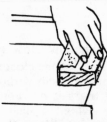

Stiff Drawers

Damp weather may cause furniture drawers to stick. If this happens, try rubbing the bottom of the drawer which glides along the inside frame with soap or candlewax. It will also help if you rub the sides with sandpaper.

Keeping Out Cold

To prevent cold air from coming in through cracks at the top, bottom and middle portion of your windows, open the window, place folded cloth or newspaper at those points, and close the window tightly. This will make for an instant, tight seal.

Frost-free Windows

To keep frost from forming on your windows in cold weather, rub the outside with alcohol or salt water and then polish the surface with newspaper.

Part Two

Floors, Walls, and Ceilings

━━━━━━━━━━━━━━━━━━━━━━━━━━━━━━

Holes in Linoleum

Small holes in linoleum can be mended with a thick paste made of finely chopped-up cork mixed with shellac. As soon as the mixture has hardened in the hole, sandpaper the surface smooth. Touch up with a closely matching paint.

Broken Linoleum

Using a sharp knife, make a clean cut and remove the broken section of linoleum. Cut a new section to fit the area that was removed. To get an exact fit, mark the area with tracing paper and trace outline onto the linoleum (using carbon paper). Cement the new section into place. Don't nail down the broken section. Nails will only pop-up in the future and become a hazard.

Cracked Ceilings and Walls

Ceilings and walls may be so badly cracked that a great deal of patching is required before you can start painting. You can avoid all that work by using a textured plaster-like material that hides cracks

and other blemishes. It is a heavy, vinyl-compound mix that rolls on

easily (with a deep-nap roller), and produces a surface that diffuses light pleasantly. The surface can be painted. Your paint dealer will be able to advise you.

Holes in Floors

Holes in wooden floors can be filled with wood putty or plastic wood. Either filler can be sanded, and can be stained to match the floor.

Holes in Plasterboard

A large hole in a plasterboard wall can be repaired by cutting out a rectangular portion tall enough to include the entire hole and wide enough to reach from the middle of one stud to the middle of the next one. (If your contractor followed building-code rules, studs should be 16 inches distant, from the center of one stud to the center of the next one.) A new piece of plasterboard, exactly the same size and thickness as the broken portion that was removed, is placed over the new opening and nailed at the ends to the partially exposed studs.

Secure the new section with plasterboard nail-heads driven in sufficiently so they do not protrude. Use a nail-set to be sure they are below the surface of the plasterboard. Fill in the edges of the newly inserted piece with a prepared mixture of plaster available in all hardware stores (such as Spackle). Then cover the mix with two-inch paper tape and smooth out with a three-inch scraper. When dry, sand the area and paint. If the wall is not smooth add more plaster-mix and smooth out as above.

Panel Adhesive

The adhesive applied to the backs of wall panels has a neoprene (synthetic rubber) base, and is so strong that only a small amount need be used. The adhesive comes in cartridges which can be used with any inexpensive caulking gun. Cut the nozzle of the cartridge at a slant to allow a ½-inch bead to come out. Place a continuous bead all around the perimeter of the panel approximately ½-inch from the edge. Then make an X with the adhesive across the back of the panel. This will be enough adhesive to make the panel adhere firmly to the plasterboard.

Nailing Down Paneling

To protect your paneling when hammering nails into it, drill a small hole into a piece of formica and slide it over the nail. If you miss the nail, you won't hit the paneling. When the nail is flush with the wood strip,

remove the wood and drive in the nail with a nail-set.

Holes in Wood Paneling

Nail holes, small cracks, and other minor imperfections in wood paneling can be made almost invisible with the aid of colored putty sticks, available wherever wall paneling is sold. The sticks consist of a soft waxy material that can be applied directly to the hole or crack.

Mixing Plaster

Add the plaster to the water, not the water to the plaster. It is much easier to work that way. Of course with ready-to-use plaster products now available (such as Spackle), there is hardly any need to bother mixing your own.

Slow-drying Plaster

Plaster that hardens too fast is difficult to work with. To retard the drying of the plaster you are using, add a few drops of vinegar to the mixture.

Plastering Corner Cracks

Deep corner cracks are quite common to the rooms of older houses. The best way to repair these cracks is to remove all loose plaster, and then cover the area with a thin film of plaster. (Ready-made plaster is available in all hardware and paint stores under trade names such as Spackle.) Fold a length of perforated tape in the center and lay it into the plaster.

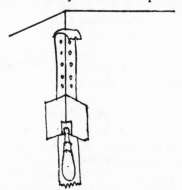

Press it into the plaster with your fingers. Next, spread more plaster over the tape until it is fully covered by plaster. Smooth with a corner trowel. In a few hours, after the plaster has dried, sand the area until the outer edges of the plaster blend in smoothly with the rest of the wall surface. You are now ready to paint or re-paper the area.

Driving Nails Into Plaster

When nails are driven into plaster, plaster often will crack. Here are a few suggestions that should be helpful:

1. Heat the nail first and it will go in more smoothly—and without dislodging a chunk of plaster in the process.
2. Hit the nail into the wall at a 45° angle (approximately).
3. Apply a small piece of tape (scotch tape or electrical tape) and drive in nail (preferably at an angle). The tape can be removed immediately and the wall will remain unblemished.

Plaster Drippings

Plaster that has dripped and fallen on painted surfaces can be removed by rubbing with steel wool. Light rubbing will prevent damage to the underlying surface. Traces of plaster that still remain can be dissolved by rubbing with a solution of lemon juice and water: one part lemon juice and three parts water.

Scratched Woodwork

Deeply scratched woodwork can be filled with a mixture of fine sawdust and spar varnish. When the filler has hardened, smooth it with fine sandpaper. Woodwork with only light scratches can be sanded and varnished.

Contact Paper

Having contact paper stick to a surface before it's in place is often a nuisance. Avoid the problem by rubbing the sticky side very lightly with a damp, sudsy sponge. The paper will slide into place easily, after which you can smooth it, and it will stick without any problem.

Part Three

Restoring Furniture and Floor Coverings

＊＊＊＊＊＊＊＊＊＊＊＊＊＊＊＊＊＊＊＊＊＊

Gluing Guidance

To avoid having the glue spill over onto other nearby objects or sticking to the surface on which you are working, spread out a length of waxed paper and do your gluing on it. If the glued objects must be weighted to keep them securely together while the glue is drying, there is a good probability that the glue will seep out onto the piece you are using for a weight. Keeping waxed paper under the weight will save you a great deal of clean-up time.

Glue Container Tops

Glues, shellacs or other adhesives usually adhere to the top of the container in which they are stored, and it is often difficult to open them. Spread petroleum jelly (vaseline) over the parts of the lid that touch the container. The glue will not stick to those areas, and you will have no difficulty in opening the container.

Softening Glue

Most glues that have hardened can usually be softened by adding a few drops of vinegar to the container in which the glue is stored.

Glue Application

When it is required to cover a large surface with a thin coat of glue uniformly spread, use a fine-toothed comb to spread the glue. The comb-spreader is especially useful when working on non-porous surfaces like veneer.

Gluing Clamps

To hold glued object while drying, use spring-type clothes pins and paper clips. If these are not available, use the clamps that can be found on some clothes hangers.

Gluing Glass

When gluing one glass surface to another glass surface, shellac is an excellent adhesive. First, set the shellac in an old dish and put a match to it. This will burn up and get rid of the alcohol. What is left will be an excellent adhesive that can be used to join glass to glass, and leather to metal, plus many other combinations of materials.

Gluing Metal to Wood

When gluing metal to wood, first saturate the metal surface with acetone, which is available in hardware and paint stores. When the acetone has dried, join the metal to the wood with a regular household cement.

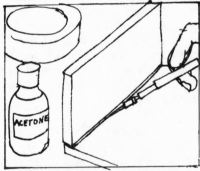

Gluing Plastic and Plexiglass

When applied to plastic surfaces, acetone will dissolve the plastic enough to allow the pieces to bond. Set the plastic or plexiglass on a secure foundation and tape the parts to be joined in place. To apply the acetone, you will need a glass or metal applicator, such as a hypodermic needle. (A plastic needle would dissolve.) Apply the acetone to the edges where the two pieces meet. Leave the tape in place until the melted plastic has set firmly.

Mending Chinaware and Glass

Broken chinaware and glass objects can be mended with most household cements. To hold the pieces in place while the glue is drying, use modeling clay. Force the modeling clay against the pieces being glued so that they will keep the glued parts from moving while the glue is drying.

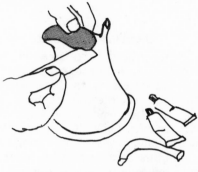

Gluing Ceramic Pieces

Epoxy resin glue is the proper adhesive to use for fixing ceramic pieces. The glue comes in two separate tubes or containers: one with resin and one with hardener. These must be thoroughly mixed. Be certain that the pieces being glued are especially clean.

Repairing Holes in Plastic

To mend holes in plastic items, such as buckets and toys, start by sanding the area around the hole. This will roughen the area so the bond will be stronger. Place another piece of plastic, preferably of the same type, over the hole and use a soldering iron set on low heat. First, dip the tip of the soldering iron in oil, then fuse the patch to the plastic being repaired.

The plastic inside lining of the caps of most aspirin bottles, and the plastic covers of coffee and peanut cans are good for patching small holes.

Repairing Torn Canvas

Canvas articles can be repaired with rubber cement. Hold the patch (which should also be canvas material) in place, and apply a weight to it after cementing. Leave the weight on the patch for several hours.

Fixing Furniture Joints

When glued furniture joints begin to loosen, it's time to re-glue. It's not necessary to disassemble the piece to do the job. Pull the joint slightly apart and apply the glue with an eyedropper. Warm the glue beforehand for easier spreading by placing its container in hot water for a few minutes. Tie rope at proper points and tie a strong knot to hold together furniture until glue has dried.

Tightening Loose Casters

Casters will wobble when they fit loosely in their sockets. You can easily correct this by removing them from their sockets and wrapping the stems with aluminum foil. Crinkle the foil a bit to create a rougher surface which will hold better. Use several turns of foil, if necessary.

Squeaky Chairs

The same silicone lubricant that is recommended to take the creak out of door hinges can be used to take the squeak out of chairs. The lubricant is packaged in aerosol cans and available at hardware stores. Spray a small amount of the lubricant directly at the point where the tops of the legs meet the seat of the chair—and also on the spots where crossbars meet the legs.

Scratched Mahogany

You can hide scratches on your mahogany furniture by using ordinary iodine as a touch-up. Apply with the end of a match or toothpick. Polish when dry. If the iodine is darker than the mahogany, lighten it with a drop or two of rubbing alcohol.

Scratched Walnut

Shallow scratches in the finish of walnut furniture can be concealed by rubbing the scratches with the meat or kernel of a walnut. The natural oil in the walnut will darken the scratches, and they will become almost invisible to the naked eye. After applying the kernel, dry off with a clean cloth.

Blistered Veneer

To repair blistered veneer, cut away the blister by making a slit all around it with a razor blade. The incision should be made parallel to the grain of the wood. Next, cover the area with a cloth moistened in hot water, and leave the cloth in place until the veneer softens. Quickly, apply stainproof glue to the area beneath the raised blister, using the blade of a knife. Then cover the blister with waxed paper and press flat with a heavy weight to hold the blister down until the glue dries. Scrape off the glue that oozes out and apply a fresh coat of furniture polish or wax.

Burns in Furniture

To remove burns like those

caused by cigarettes, obtain powdered pumice from your hardware or paint store. Wrap a piece of felt around a wooden block and tack it down. Dip it in water and squeeze almost dry. Sprinkle the powdered pumice on the burned area and rub lightly. If the area that has the burn is very small, wrap the felt around your fingertip and rub gently.

Cigarette Burns in Upholstery

Use a yarn in a color that closely matches the upholstery. Darn over the burned area with small, close-together stitches. Then iron the patched area through a damp cloth.

Steel Sandpaper

A piece of thin steel—tempered and of high quality—can do a better job than sandpaper—and it is easier to work and cheaper in the long run. Usually called cabinet scrapers, the flat, thin (about 1/16 inch), scrapers usually are 2 inches by 6 inches. Specialty hardware stores carry them in a few other sizes and shapes. You can scrape and smooth with them—and they work on wood, plasterboard and most any other surface.

Drawer Gliders

Drawers in wooden chests and bureaus often stick in warm, humid weather. Since the cause of the sticking is the swelling of the drawer, sandpapering its runners will help reduce its size. After sandpapering, wax the runners with a piece of ordinary candle. Drive thumb tacks into the lower part of the drawer opening, one on each side where the drawer runners can ride over them. This should make the drawer slide easily.

Unfinished Furniture

Finishing unfinished furniture can be pleasurable provided the wood is of reasonably good quality. Furniture made of kiln-dried wood is less likely to shrink or warp. If the piece you select does have knots you should make certain they are firm and tight and are not likely to fall out. Avoid furniture with too many knots. Watch out for blue-gray streaks which indicate the presence of mildew or some other fungus. These cannot be bleached out easily, if at all, and may show through even after applying several coats of paint.

Balancing Furniture Legs

A perfectly balanced table or chair, when moved to a new spot, may rock and be unsteady. The fault is not in the chair, but in the floor. Nevertheless, you will have to adjust the chair leg lengths to solve your problem. One way is to pack plastic wood or ordinary glazing putty under the "short" leg. Before applying, place a piece of waxed paper between the leg and the floor to prevent the putty or plastic wood from sticking to the floor. If the table or chair is later moved to a spot where the shim is not needed, it can be cut loose with a sharp knife.

Another solution is to attach a piece of wood of the correct thickness and size to the bottom of the leg. Nail it in place with thin brads which can be easily removed.

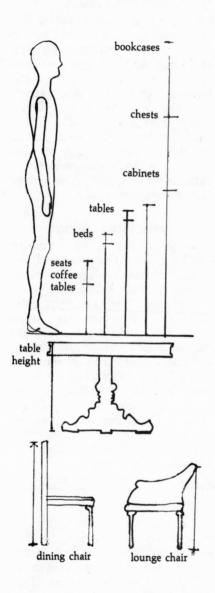

have been tested and proven, and that will provide the greatest comfort. Chairs are about 17 inches to the seat, on an average; coffee tables are 12 inches-13 inches; tables are 29 inches-30 inches.

Stripping Furniture

Stripping old finishes from furniture is easier and inexpensive when you use common household lye. Dilute the lye first by adding about six ounces to 1½ quarts of water. Any container is fine except aluminum, which will be corroded by the lye. After stirring the mixture slowly, apply it to the furniture with a brush or sponge, allow it to set, then rinse. Wear gloves and long sleeves during the process, as lye will burn the skin. If any lye does spatter on you, wash the area immediately and thoroughly with plenty of water.

Removing Decals

To remove a decal without damaging the surface beneath, cover the decoration with a wet washcloth and press a hot iron to the cloth. In a few minutes steam will loosen the decal.

Holes in Carpets

Scraps of carpeting left over after laying a new carpet will come in handy at a later date when you have to repair holes, especially those made by flying sparks from the fireplace or from dropped cigarettes. When preparing to fill a hole, shave off some of the nap from the carpet scrap, mix it with transparent glue, and then carefully fill in the hole.

Building Furniture

If you are planing to make your own furniture such as tables, chairs, cabinets and chests, follow the standard measurements that

134

Part Four

Interior Remodeling and Decorating

Locating Studs

When correctly spaced, the two-by-fours (called *studs*) that stand

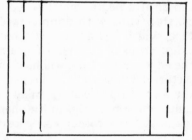

vertically inside all walls are 16 inches apart. This means that the distance from the *center* of one stud to the *center* of the next stud is 16 inches. It is helpful to know this when you want to hang heavy mirrors, shelves or decorative objects on a wall. It is best to drive nails or screws into studs if the article you are hanging is heavy.

Hanging Pictures

Standard picture hooks are safe and efficient. The smallest size available will hold a picture weigh-

ing up to 15 pounds, the largest will support 50 pounds. Before hammering the nail into the wall, place a small piece of adhesive or cloth tape on the spot where the nail is to enter the wall. The tape will prevent the wall from cracking. Place the hook (with the nail in position in the slot) flat against the wall, tap the head of the nail with your ham-

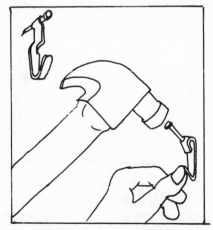

mer and drive the nail all the way in. The angle will be right to give the picture all the support required.

picture from falling suddenly, something that happens from time to time with frames. You should have no trouble making the type of knot shown here.

Fading Pictures

You can retard the fading of your framed pictures by making sure that air circulates behind the picture. You can accomplish this by seeing to it that the lower corners of the frame are held away from the wall through the use of carpet tacks or some such device.

Hanging Pictures Straight

To test whether a picture is truly straight, suspend a weight, such as a nut or bolt, from one end of a string and hold it against the wall, allowing it to hang freely. The string will form a true straight line, and you can adjust the picture accordingly.

Two-faced Tape

Pictures with lightweight frames, as well as mounted but unframed photographs and pictures, can be attached to metal, wood or plaster walls with double-faced tape, which has adhesive on both sides. Strips of tape placed around the edges of the back will hold the picture if it is pressed firmly against the wall. Larger pictures may require additional strips in the shape of an X from corner to opposite corner.

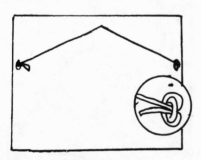

Unframed Pictures

If you have unframed, valuable pieces of art, make sure your hands are clean before handling them. Smudges can often be difficult to remove. When lifting unframed pictures, use both hands to avoid tearing and be sure nothing rubs across the surface. You can make your own storage folder by folding a 32 × 40-inch two-ply cardboard in half, then taping one end with linen tape.

Picture Knot

The kind of knot you tie when putting the cord or wire through the rings on the back of your picture frame is important. The proper kind of knot will keep your

Watercolors

To preserve your watercolor paintings, place them between pieces of glass, but do not varnish or spray-coat paintings. Watercolors are especially vulnerable to light, water spots, and moisture. Should a valuable watercolor become soiled or damaged, take it to a restorer instead of trying to remedy the problem yourself.

Pastel Drawings

Drawings executed with crayon, chalk, charcoal and the like should be kept under glass, separated from direct contact with the glass by a mat or strip. Do not use an acrylic cover, as its static electricity may literally "pick up" your picture. Handle pastels gently. Sudden movement can shock the colors right off their background. Since pastels are tricky to clean, leave this task to an expert.

Oil Paintings

Whether oils have been executed on a canvas background or on wood, handle them with care. If the painting is on wood, be extremely careful about transferring it to a new location because changes in the atmosphere will cause wood to expand or contract. When your oil needs a cleaning, it is best to leave the task to a professional.

Cleaning Paintings

It is wise to dust oil paintings regularly and to brush them every few months with a clean, soft brush. Do not use a cloth on the painting. The glass covering the picture can be wiped with a cloth dampened with window cleaner, but do not spray the cleaning agent directly on the glass. Droplets might run down and get into the picture itself. When cleaning acrylic covers, use a cloth dampened slightly with a solution of mild detergent and water.

Art and Insects

Some insects are attracted to the ingredients in works of art. Silverfish, termites, cockroaches, and woodworms are particularly fond of paste, glue sizing, and wood pulp paper. Inspect the backs of frames occasionally for insect damage, even if you have not seen evidence of their presence. When attack by insects becomes a persistent problem, call in a commercial exterminator, and be sure to tell him to use insecticides that will not stain paper, reminding him that your works of art are valuable.

Artwork Restoration

Good restorers of damaged artwork, sometimes called "conservators," can work miracles in fixing damaged and deteriorated art. They can remove brown spots or foxing, clean watercolors and prints, repair cracks and checks (hairline splits which may be only in the varnish on an oil painting). They can prevent further cracking and can also disguise actual stains that cannot be removed. A good place to seek advice on who to call in to do your restoration work is at a university art department, or from a museum curator.

Picture Frame Repairs

Chipped sections of a wooden frame can usually be successfully repaired with one of the many fillers available in powder form at hardware stores. Mix the powder with a small amount of water to make a heavy paste, and add to the chipped portion of the frame shape as required. It will dry quickly and be ready for sanding, carving and staining within two hours.

Loose Picture Nails

If the nail holding your picture has become loose, wrap a thin strip of adhesive tape around the nail shaft and dip it in glue. Force the taped nail into the enlarged hole, and allow the nail to dry in the hole for a day before rehanging the picture. Or, if you have plaster handy, you can simply refill the hole with new plaster, allow it to harden, and then hammer the nail into the wall.

Wall Paneling and Pre-planning

Before installing tongue-and-groove wall paneling check the color of the tongues and groove edges. If they are lighter than the color of the panel surface, darken them with a stain or paint to match the shade of the panel. Darkening them is necessary because sometimes the panels shrink and some of the edges are revealed.

Handling Paneling

Cutting a hole in the precise spot for electrical outlet or switches in wood paneling is tricky, and a slight mistake may ruin a whole panel. One way of proceeding is to coat the edges of the outlet with lipstick or chalk and to place the panel in the proper position with its back against the outlet. Tap the panel against the outlet with a rubber mallet or an ordinary hammer, using a block of wood to protect the panel surface. The outline of the outlet will then appear on the back of the panel and serve as an accurate guide for cutting the opening.

See-through Shelves

When you store things on the top shelves of a closet, it is practically impossible to see the articles unless you are over 6' 6" in height. One way to overcome the difficulty is to replace the wood shelves with see-through shelves of glass or plastic so you can see from below what you have stored above.

Lining Shelves

If you have a shelf on which you keep light objects (like empty jars) that tend to slide around, you might want to try lining that particular shelf with sheets of sandpaper. The very lightest grade of sandpaper or emery paper will do the trick.

Plastic Storm-Windows

To make your own storm-window, measure the size of the window. Cut an over-sized piece of heavyweight see-through plastic, large enough so that you can double-up the plastic around the outer moldings of the window. Tack or staple through the bunching, around the window's edge. It will provide a good airtight seal that will keep your house warmer and reduce your heating bills.

Replacing Floor Tiles

Floor tiles bond extremely well and are difficult to remove once firmly pressed in place. If it is necessary to replace a broken or damaged tile, place aluminum foil over the tile to be removed, then heat the area with a hot iron. The adhesive beneath the tile will soften. Use a putty knife to lift the tile beneath the seams. Pry the tile loose from the floor. If the adhesive is still not soft, use additional heat to soften it.

Fitting Border Tiles

When fitting the last row of floor tile against the wall, the best method of measuring the size to which

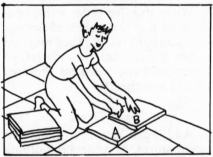

the tile should be cut is to place a loose tile (figure A) over a tile already set in the next row. Place a second loose tile (figure B) against the wall, the outer edge overlapping tile A. Where the outer edge of tile B ends, draw a line against tile A with a pencil. Cut with scissors or knife along the line. Remove the cut-off and slide tile A against the wall.

Fitting Linoleum Tiles Around Obstructions

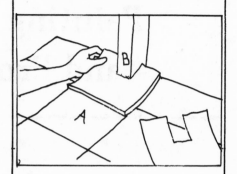

To fit a linoleum tile around an obstruction, first lay a piece of paper the same size as the tile along the edge of the tile already in place in the next row (Figure A). Slide the paper to the edge of the obstruction (Figure B) and mark the width of the obstruction on the paper with a pencil. Then, mark the depth of the obstruction against the far sides of the paper. Mark a point on each side of the paper indicating the depth and draw a line joining the two points. Extend the width lines of the paper model until they meet the depth line. Cut away the enclosed area representing the obstruction. Fit the paper model against the obstruction to be sure it fits. If the paper pattern fits perfectly, then the tile should also. Trace the outline of the pattern on a loose tile and cut out the tile.

Part Five

Painting Products and Procedures

─•──•──•──•──•──•──•──•──•──•──•──•──•──•──•─

Electric Paint Mixer

Mixing paint properly is a time-consuming job. With an electric drill and a special paint mixer attachment that is inserted like a drill bit, you can save time and get a more thorough mix. The paint-bit-mixer is available in most hardware stores. Dip it in the can of paint before starting the drill motor, and do not remove it from the paint can until the twirling motion stops. This will avoid paint spatter.

Color Durability

White paint is the most durable of all colors. The lighter the color of the paint, the less slowly it will fade. Dark shades fade much more quickly.

For Brighter Rooms

When you redecorate, paint walls in light pastel colors and ceilings in a white or off-white tint. Use a flat or semi-gloss paint on walls and ceilings to help diffuse the light and make the room appear brighter.

Painting Basement Walls

When painting cellar walls, bear in mind that there is an advantage to using light colors. They may soil more quickly, but they do reflect more light and will keep the area bright and cheerful.

Japan Dryer

Add japan dryer, available in paint stores, to control the drying speed of paint. Use less on warm days, more on cold days.

Linseed Oil as Thinner

Linseed oil is an excellent wood preservative. This is why it's a good idea to thin outdoor paint with it, rather than using turpentine as a thinner. Turpentine tends to evaporate and does not help the wood. Linseed oil restores some of the wood's original vitality.

Paint Brush Shampoo

Cleaning paint brush bristles with turpentine or paint thinner is only the first step if you want to preserve your brushes. To complete the job, give the bristles a thorough shampoo. Scrub them in a solution of one part liquid shampoo to three parts water. When the bristles get foamy, the residue is gone. Rinse the bristles thoroughly in warm water and hang the brushes up to dry.

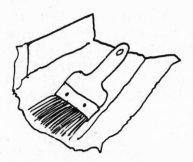

Paint-can Drip

Each time you press a paint brush against the rim of a can to clean off excess paint, the groove around the rim of the can catches some of the paint, unless you are extremely careful. In time, the paint runs down the side of the can. Avoid the drip by punching several holes in the bottom of the groove that runs around the can into which the lid fits. The excess paint will flow back into the can and resealing of the lid will not be affected because the lid seals against the sides and not the bottom of the groove.

Keeping Brushes Soft I

It's not necessary to clean a paint

brush if you are going to use it the next day. Sprinkle a few drops of turpentine or linseed on it and wrap it tightly in aluminum foil or wax paper. Store the brush flat.

Keeping Brushes Soft II

You can avoid cleaning a brush you plan to use again shortly by drilling a hole in its handle and suspending it in the paint can. Insert a long thin dowel (or curtain rod) through the hole. The hole in the brush handle should be made in

two or three spots so that the rod can be inserted at the right spot to keep the bristles of the brush from touching the bottom of the can.

141

Keeping Brushes Soft III

A paint brush can be kept soft between coats of paint without being thoroughly cleaned by pouring about two inches of paint thinner into a tall coffee can with a

plastic lid. Cut an X in the center of the lid. Exercise the brush a bit in the thinner, then push the handle through the X in the plastic lid. Adjust the handle so that the bristles are covered by thinner but do not touch the bottom of the can. When ready to paint again, just wipe the bristles with a rag and start painting.

Keeping Brushes Soft IV

When refinishing furniture or doing a job requiring repeated coats of varnish or paint remover, you can avoid the bother of having to clean the brush between coats by wrapping it in aluminum foil and putting it into your freezer.

Touch-up Paint

It is wise to save the leftover paint after finishing a room or an article of furniture. You never know when you may wish you had just a little bit of paint to touch up a marred surface. For such touch-up jobs, instead of a brush, use the kind of applicators doctors use to swab throats. You can make your own by twirling some cotton around the tip of a toothpick or a wooden dowel.

Screening Paint

If film has formed on the surface of your paint, or if your paint looks lumpy, remove the hardened film with a piece of wood or a wide blade. Then stretch a nylon stock-

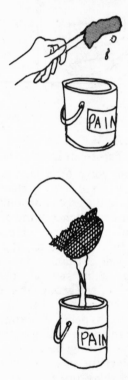

ing or nylon screening across the opening of the can and strain the paint into a clean can. Metal screening can be used as well.

Cleaning Paint Rollers

Because paint rollers are designed to hold fluids, it is often difficult to get all the rinse water out of them after they have been cleaned.

Whirling the roller from an electric drill is one good way to get rid of the excess water quickly. To prepare the drill buy a length of ¼-inch threaded steel rod at a hardware store. Cut the rod with a hacksaw so that the piece is 2½ inches longer than the roller. Put the rod through the roller and add a washer and butterfly nut at each end of the roller. Tighten the nut, and select a location where spattering water will not create a problem. Put one

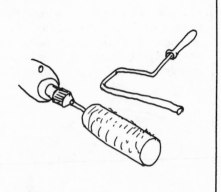

end of the rod in the chuck of your drill, close the chuck and turn on the drill.

Storing a Paint Roller

If you are undertaking a paint job that will last for several days, an easy way to keep the paint roller in good, usable condition is to store the entire roller assembly, including the roller and the tray with paint in it, in an *airtight* plastic bag. Before putting the assembly in a plastic bag, roll the roller in the paint that is in the tray so as to moisten the nap. This will keep the roller soft and fresh for the next time you use it, whether it's a day or a month later. This type of storage will save you the trouble of cleaning rollers and the expense of buying new ones.

Cleaning Paint Trays

Paint roller trays are a nuisance to clean even when water-based (latex) paints have been used in them. And the job is extremely messy when you have used an oil-based paint. One way to solve the problem is to line the tray with heavy-duty aluminum foil. If you allow the foil to overlap on all four sides by at least one inch, the final clean-up will be easy. Simply pour off remaining paint, remove the foil, and the tray will be ready for use again.

Paint Roller Nap

The nap on paint rollers comes in various thicknesses. To paint smooth surfaces (like most indoor walls), use the shortest, least bulky nap available. For slightly textured surfaces, a medium length nap is best. To cover rough, heavily textured surfaces, use a roller with a long nap. Long nap rollers are also best suited for irregular surfaces like wood shakes (shingles) and chain link fences.

Bucket-holder for Painting Equipment

Laying a paint brush across the top of a can of paint is a dangerous practice, especially when painting on a ladder or scaffold. The brush may get knocked off and land in the paint or fall on the floor and make an awful mess.

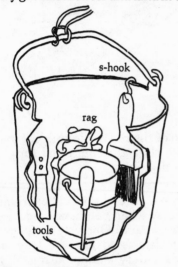

To avoid trouble, place the can of paint in a larger-size bucket. Attach an S-hook to the rim of the bucket (see illustration) and hang the brush so that, when not in use, it is positioned between the can and bucket. Any dripping from the brush will drop to the bottom of the bucket, and the floor will never get messed up. You may have to drill a larger hole in the top of the paint brush handle in order to accommodate the hook.

You can also use the bucket as a convenient place to keep a paint scraper, a putty knife, or a rag. You can either lay these articles in the bucket or hang them from additional S-hooks. The bucket or pail can hang from a hook attached to the ladder.

Leftover Paint

Small amounts of paint left over when the job is finished should not be left in a large can. If poured into a smaller can, the surface area will be reduced and, consequently, the less paint skin will be formed.

Avoid Splattering Paint

You can avoid splattering paint which often occurs when you seal a paint can by punching holes in the rim of the can with a nail or an awl. The paint that accumulates in the rim will drip into the can, and the cover will still make a tight seal. An even simpler method of avoiding splattering is to cover the lid of the can with a piece of cloth that hangs over the sides. Hammer the lid gently, using soft blows around the circumference of the lid.

The Paint-skin Bypass

Skin that covers the surface of paint in paint cans not used for a while is often a great nuisance and takes up precious time when you have to remove it. A simple way of tackling the problem is to close the lid tightly on such cans you do not plan to use shortly, and to then store the cans in an upside down position. When you open the can the next time you use the paint, you will find whatever skin has formed is on the *bottom*, not on the top.

Preventing Paint Skin

You can prevent skin from forming on paint in a resealed can by pouring some turpentine on the surface of the paint. Cover the can

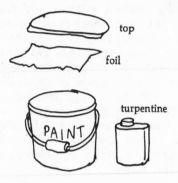

top

foil

turpentine

PAINT

with aluminum foil and then press the lid on tightly.

Containers for Mixing Paint

Quart and half-gallon milk containers are extremely useful for mixing small quantities of paint and stain and it is wise to keep a number on hand for future use. Cut away the top of the container, leaving anywhere from one to five inches of the bottom section. If you are going to work with a larger amount of stain or paint you should cut the container to a height of four or five inches. Select a container that will accommodate the full width of the brush you are planning to use.

Jar Lids as Containers

Lids from jars of coffee, peanut butter or mayonnaise are worth

saving because they can be used as containers for mixing small quantities of epoxies, or glue that is being mixed with sawdust, or for touch-up paint. Once used, there is no need to clean them or reuse them, since they are so readily available.

Shower Curtain Dropcloths

An old shower curtain that has become discolored or whose eyelets are torn need not be discarded. Lay it away as is, and save it for "painting day." It is not only heavier than the plastic dropcloths available today at paint stores, but is, in fact, more durable.

Reducing Paint Odors

If the odor of paint is more than you can bear, take time to add vanilla extract to your paint. Add two teaspoons of extract to each quart.

Sandpapering Before Painting

A sandpapered surface offers a better grip for paint, and retards the cracking and blistering of the paint. Sandpaper also removes dirt and grease and permits the paint to go on more easily. A product called Liquid Sandpaper which can be applied with a cloth very easily, is available in paint stores.

Sanding With Pumice

Before starting to sandpaper, sprinkle some fine pumice on the painted surface. This will keep the paint from clogging the sandpaper. Because the pumice is abrasive, you'll do the job that much faster, and the sandpaper will last longer.

Protective Measures I

Save those large plastic bags you get from the dry cleaners. They are ideal for protecting hanging lamps and chandeliers from sanding and dripping when you work on the ceiling. The most effective way of protecting ceiling fixtures is to release the cover plate that is screwed

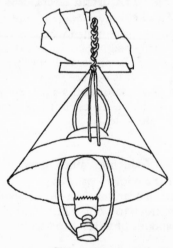

into the ceiling, and let it slide down the chain. Pull the plastic sack up over the entire unit and tie a cord around it as high up on the chain as you can.

Protective Measures II

If you do not have a dropcloth handy when painting, the plastic bags from the cleaners, as well as

ordinary plastic bags used for the trash, can be cut open and spread out over all the furniture and the floors. Remove your shoes when working, so when you walk on the plastic bags you will not tear them.

Paint Stripping

When removing the finish from old furniture with jellied paint stripper, remember to wear rubber gloves, and you will not run the risk of burning your hands. Do not use plastic gloves because some plastics are easily dissolved by paint stripper. When stripping paint, always work in a well-ventilated area since the fumes can be quite toxic. Above all, do not smoke while working, because most paint strippers are highly flammable.

Paint-stripper Evaporation

Paint strippers contain highly volatile solvents that evaporate rapidly. The longer the solvents remain moist, the better they do the job of removing the finish. To delay the evaporation of the solvents, place a sheet of waxed paper over the jellied stripper, wait about an hour, then remove the sludge with a scraper.

Removing Paint Sludge

After paint stripper has been applied to a surface, allow it to stand for a while. Then, dust the surface lightly with sawdust, or woodshavings, or excelsior. Next, use a dry rag to remove the stripper. The sawdust and woodshavings increase the friction on the normally slippery surface and make removal of the sludge much easier.

Painting Procedure

When painting a room start at the upper right-hand corner and work down. Try to finish each day's work at a corner or near a window so as to prevent overlaps when you resume painting. Paint one wall at a time.

Painting Platform

When you plan to paint a wall or ceiling (or if you want to hang curtains) you will have to reach up for an extended period of time. Save wear and tear on yourself by making a platform to stand on. Use two kitchen chairs of the same size, and lay a board of 12 inches or more across the two seats. The longer and wider the board, the better. You will have more mobility and your platform will be more secure.

Painting Stairs

A clever way of painting stairs is to paint every other stair so that you can walk up and down on the unpainted steps. When the painted

stairs are dry, paint the unpainted ones and you'll still be able to use the stairs while the paint's drying.

Painting a Floor

Save a backache, and instead of a paint brush use a new pushbroom with soft bristles when painting a floor. Put the paint in a shallow pan large enough to accommodate the broom.

Painting Cabinet Knobs

Knobs of cabinets can be spray-painted easily and quickly without getting any paint on your fingers. First, remove the knob and its screw from the cabinet. Then turn the screw into the knob only partway. Next, place the knob on a bottle with a narrow neck. The screw should face the bottom of the bottle. The neck of the bottle will serve as a support while you are painting, and the bottle can be turned as required without getting paint on your fingers. The knob can be left on the bottle until completely dry.

Shellac Before Painting

If you want good, even coverage when painting your walls, coat them first with shellac to assure even absorption of the paint. Use fresh shellac, since it dries very quickly and you will be able to paint the walls the same day you shellac them. Even better results will be assured, and you will prevent peeling, if you can afford the time to remove all the old paint before applying the shellac.

Re-painting Linoleum

Worn out lineoleum can be given a new lease on life. Special linoleum paint is available and requires only ordinary application. After the paint has dried, cover the area with a coat of wax.

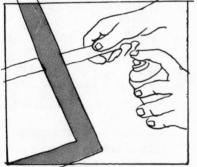

Painting Picture Frames

It is easy to paint picture frames without getting finger marks on them, and without getting paint on your hands. Simply attach a slim piece of wood to the back of the frame with small, thin nails (brads). The wood pieces should extend three or four inches beyond the frame on each side. The extended wood will serve as a handle by which you can move the frame around as you proceed with the painting. After you finish painting one part you can turn the frame in any direction to reach the next part without touching the freshly painted portions.

Painting on Brass

A brass surface must be carefully prepared if paint is to adhere to it. First wash the brass with a household cleaner that does not contain soap. Then, wipe the surface with denatured alcohol and proceed with the painting.

Painting Flowerpots

Painting a flowerpot is a simple procedure if you place the pot upside down on a can tall enough to raise the pot above the surface on which you are doing the job. Protect the surface with old newspapers to catch paint that drips.

Painting Metal Surfaces

It is not always easy to apply paint to the metal surfaces of wastepaper baskets and garbage cans. To make painting easier, and to make sure the paint adheres, clean the surface thoroughly first,

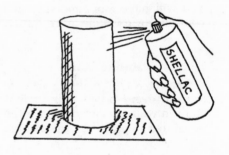

then spray it with shellac. When the shellac is dry, apply the paint.

Painting Stripes

Paint stripes of any width and any length can be made perfectly with masking tape and an aerosol spray can of paint. First, clean the surface of all dirt, dust, oil and grease. Place masking tape strips in parallel lines spaced as desired. Measure with a ruler so lines will be straight. Protect the surrounding wall by taping newspaper over it. Spray the area between the tapes,

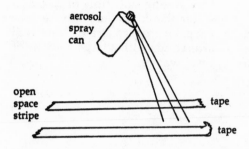

aerosol spray can

open space stripe

tape

tape

holding the spray can about 12 inches from the surface. Lift tapes before paint is entirely dry to avoid ragged edges caused by chipping of hardened paint.

Knots That Bleed

Knots in lumber such as pine, hemlock, or fir often contain resin that "bleeds" through white or light-colored paints. Stains appear in the form of brownish rings. If this happens, cover the brown spots with four-pound cut white shellac. When the shellac has dried, sand the surface lightly with fine sandpaper, wipe clean, and paint. White, pigmented, shellac primer can also be used.

Paint-sealed Windows

For windows that have been painted and cannot be opened because paint has hardened, a special tool is available at hardware and paint stores. Sometimes called a window zipper or zip tool, it has fine, sharp teeth to cut through paint film. Of course, you should first try a two- or three-inch wide plastering spatula which will usually loosen a window that has been painted shut.

Staining Without Brushes

You can save the effort, nuisance and cost of handling messy brushes by using cloth rags or a sponge with which to apply stain (or varnish). Dip the cloth or sponge in the stain and apply it to the wood, rubbing it in well until the stain is evenly distributed. With varnish or shellac use a light stroke, moving only in the direction of the grain.

Keeping Dust Off Varnish

Dust will have a hard time reaching the just-varnished surfaces where you want it least, if you suspend freshly varnished furniture upside down to dry.

Tea for Pine

Strong tea diluted with a bit of water is a good, low-cost stain for pine, giving an antique-like finish. When the stain is dry, apply two coats of fresh, white shellac.

Paint Spattering

Spattered paint will come off the floor if you apply nail polish remover. Let it soak in for several minutes, rub it off with a cleaning cloth, then wash the area with sudsy water. Turpentine and benzene are more commonly used to remove oil-based paints.

Remove Paint From Tiles

Paint that has spattered on tiles can be removed with a little turpentine on a cleaning cloth. To make the job easier, first remove as much as you can with a razor blade.

Paint on Brickwork

To remove spattered paint from brickwork, use another brick as a scrub brush. For concrete, use a broken piece of concrete. The dust created by the scrubbing will camouflage the faint traces of spatter that remain.

Spattered Concrete Floors

A strong solution of lye and water should do the job of removing paint from concrete. Rinse well afterwards with a large amount of clean water.

Chapter Seven

EXTERIOR MAINTENANCE AND BEAUTIFICATION

Part One

The House
and Its Care

· ·

Picking Up a Ladder at Its Balance Point

If you mark your ladder at its balance point with a stripe of paint, you will be in a position to pick it up and carry it easily with one hand, and without giving it one moment of forethought.

Shaky Ladders

It is best not to get onto a shaky ladder at all, but if you must, a C-clamp fastened to the top step can serve as a handy grip, especially

when you are leaning to one side and need the support. When you have to lean to the right, place the clamp to your left and grasp it with your left hand—and vice versa.

Skid-free Ladders

Slipping ladders cause accidents. Whether you use a ladder indoors

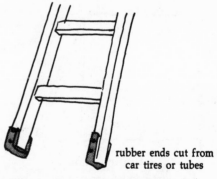

rubber ends cut from
car tires or tubes

or outdoors, if it is a ladder designed to lean against a wall, you can make it skid-free by permanently attaching to the bottom, rubber cut from old tires, old inner-tubes, or other non-skid products.

length. For example, if an extension ladder is raised to a height of 16 feet, the bottom of the ladder should be placed four feet away from the base of the wall.

Ladder Aid

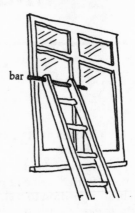

bar

Ladder Safety

Keep pieces of an old inner-tube tied to your ladder. They come in handy when your ladder has to be placed on a smooth surface. Another method of preventing slipping is to place an old asphalt shingle under each leg. The rough surface of the shingle will keep the ladder from sliding on smooth surfaces like polished floors, stone, or grass.

A ladder can serve you much better if you add a long crossbar to the top—either a one-inch round dowel (see illustration), or a piece of ¾-inch pine or plywood, four inches wide and long enough to extend two or three inches beyond the width of the window.

If you are using the round dowel, bore a 1⅛-inch hole through the two sides of the ladder about 1½ inches from the top. You can use a dowel with a wooden or an aluminum ladder. The pre-cut holes in most aluminum ladders will accept a one-inch dowel. With this support and protection, you can use the ladder to get to windows that are often difficult to reach.

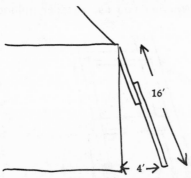

16′

4′

Positioning Ladders

Ladders can be dangerous if they are not positioned properly. If the bottom of a ladder is too close to a wall you may fall backwards. To avoid this, place the bottom of the ladder a distance from the wall equal to ¼ of the ladder's extended

Roof Ladder

If you have to get onto a sloping roof to replace a shingle, to fix the chimney, or to install a television antenna, the safest way is with the aid of a flat, wooden ladder that you

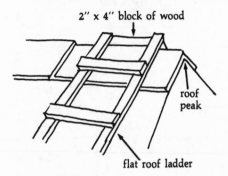

2" x 4" block of wood

roof peak

flat roof ladder

can easily nail together yourself. The important feature of the homemade roof ladder is the two-by-four block of wood that is nailed to the very *end* of the ladder. This overhanging block will hold securely over the peak of the roof and provide you with safety and mobility.

Replacing Broken Windows

When removing broken glass from a window, start by using pliers to remove glazier points.

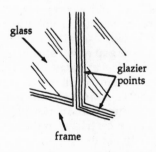

glass

glazier points

frame

When inserting the new pane, first place a thin ribbon of putty along the inside of the frame, and press the glass firmly against the putty. Insert glazier points, first near the corners, and then every four inches along the pane. Add more putty or glazing compound as needed, and smooth the surface with a putty knife. Moisten your putty knife with linseed or regular lubricating oil.

Aluminum Window Corrosion

After several years of exposure to the elements, aluminum windows become pitted and unsightly. To restore the windows, rub the frame with coarse steel wool and then complete the job with fine steel wool. A coating of zinc chromate primer followed by a good exterior enamel (white is the preferred color) will prevent the return of the gray oxide.

Metal Screens

Carpet scraps nailed to wood blocks are good for scrubbing metal screens. This is also a good way of applying varnish or shellac to screening in order to retard future corrosion. Use different blocks for the two separate operations.

Screening Holes I

Use fast-drying model airplane glue to patch small holes in window screening. It requires only a few drops to seal a hole.

Screening Holes II

For a hole in window screening large enough to require a patch, cut a section from an old piece of screening. Use fast-drying model airplane glue, and apply a bead of glue to the perimeter of the patch.

Aluminum and Copper Screening

Do not discard an aluminum or copper screen because there is a hole in it. Mend it with squares of screen patching available in various sizes in most hardware stores. Trim the torn area with metal-cutting scissors so it is square, and then select a patch larger than the new opening. Lay the patch over the hole so that the bent wires stick out on the reverse side of the screen. Then bend the protruding wires flat against the reverse side of the screen.

Patching Fiberglass Screening

A tear in fiberglass screening can be repaired with a patch of fiberglass screening a bit larger than the tear. Join the patch to the screen with heat. Have someone hold an iron frying pan to the outside of the screen while you lay the patch on the inside of the screen. Then, press a hot iron against the edges of the patch until the patch and screen fuse.

Another way to do the patching is by laying a thin bead of transparent glue (like Elmer's) along the edges of the patch before applying the heat. You should protect the iron from the glue by placing a piece of cloth over the patch before applying the heat.

Painting a Window Screen

Clean the screen itself well before beginning to paint. Use a paint roller or a clean rag to apply the paint. After painting, place the screen on a flat surface for drying so as to avoid having the paint drip into the mesh.

Caulking Out Drafts

Drafts are not only uncomfortable but add to your fuel and electricity costs. The best way to avoid this unnecessary expense is to do a good caulking job. Places most probably in need of caulking are spaces around windows where the siding butts up against the window frame, and next to door trim where two walls of different materials such as brick and wood meet.

Before adding new caulking, remove the old, dried-out caulking and clean the gap with a stiff brush. Then, place a cartridge of acrylic latex caulking in a caulking gun and apply the caulking to the gaps. Make a slanted cut in the plastic nozzle of the cartridge so that you get a bead of about ⅜ of an inch. As you work the gun, push it away from you along the edge to be filled. Choose a caulking color that matches the trim of the siding.

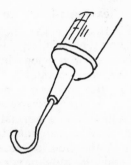

Caulking-tube Stopper

To keep caulk from oozing out of the tube when the caulking job is finished, use a section of a metal coat hanger as a stopper. Cut a three-inch piece of wire, with pliers, bend one end into a C-shape, and insert the other end into the tube. The straight end will keep the caulk from oozing out, and the hook at the other end will make it easier to slide the stopper in and out.

Homemade Cement-mix

You can make your own cement-mix that will be stronger than any you can buy pre-mixed by adding pure (Portland) cement to an equal amount of lime. Mix the cement and lime and keep it handy in a dry spot. When you have cement repair work to do add three shovels of sand to one of the cement-lime mixture. Mix them well, then add water until you reach a good consistency similar to that of mustard or mayonnaise. This cement mixture is good for filling cracks in walls, openings around pipes, and recementing loose stone or brickwork. It creates a strong bond with the old cement, especially when the crack is ¼-inch or more deep.

Loose Window Screens

Weatherstripping can make loose window screens fit snugly again. Tack the weatherstripping along the edge of the screen that fits loosely. It may be necessary to use the weatherstripping on more than one side, and test the fit. If it requires more, you can then add it to the other side.

Loose Window Panes

Loose window panes not only rattle in the wind, but allow cold air to enter in the winter and hot air in summer. To stop the rattle, and cut down on heating and air conditioning bills, apply more putty to secure the loose pane against the window frame.

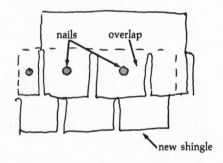

Replacing Roofing Shingles

Asphalt roofing shingles are sometimes damaged by strong winds. To replace a torn shingle, raise the shingle that overlaps it, remove the damaged shingle, and hammer down the old nails. Insert a new shingle in the position of the missing one. Drive three zinc-coated roofing nails through the tables of the overlapping shingle and the upper section of the new one. Cover the head of each nail with a spot of roofing cement about the size of a quarter.

Replacing House Shingles

Sometimes it is necessary to remove a damaged shingle. To accomplish this without damaging adjoining shingles, insert a prybar under the lower edge of the damaged piece and raise it just enough to insert the blade of a

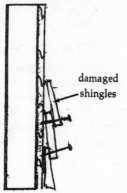

damaged shingles

small metal-cutting saw. Cut through all the nails that hold the lower edge. Then, do the same with the lower edge of the next higher shingle. The shingle can then be slipped out and a new one inserted. Drive in new nails at least one inch away from where the old ones were.

Cleaning a Fireplace Flue

If a fireplace that has always worked well suddenly begins to smoke, or if the logs burn sluggishly, you probably have an obstruction in the flue preventing the smoke from escaping through the chimney in a normal manner. Birds may have decided to make a nest in the flue, or possibly you burned old newspapers or gift wrappings and the ashes have clung to the walls of the chimney flue. Usually, the most effective solution is to tie a long rope to a sack that has been weighted with a few heavy rocks. Lower the sack down the flue, and raise it and lower it several times. This should dislodge the obstruction.

Chapped Hands

There are times when it is necessary to work out of doors in cold weather without gloves. At such times, hands should be protected from chapping. Castor oil rubbed into the hands before going outdoors and when coming back inside will offer that protection.

Chimney Downdraft Cure

The fireplace will not function properly and the house will be filled with smoke if the chimney is subject to downdrafts. Downdrafts occur when outside air is sucked into the chimney, and this can happen if the chimney is not at least two feet higher than any other part of the house roof, or if there are other obstructions nearby such as trees that are taller than the house. This can be rectified by adding two or more layers of brick to the chimney, by capping it to make a smaller opening, or by doing both. You can test whether capping will solve the problem by cutting a hole, smaller than the chimney opening, in a piece of plywood and securing it temporarily to the top of the chimney. If this smaller opening solves the problem, make a permanent opening of that size with brick or stone. If that doesn't work, extend the height of your chimney.

Fighting Wood Rot

Wood directly exposed to the earth will rot in a few years. You can delay or prevent the deterioration by using one of two chemicals on the market. One is a black liquid called creosote. It has a strong odor and stains the wood black. Wood soaked in creosote will not be attacked by termites. It cannot be painted, and the creosote should be applied with care and kept away from one's skin. The other chemical is pentachlorophenol, called "penta" for short. It likewise protects wood against decay and termites and it can be painted. Although more expensive than creosote, it has the advantage of being odorless. Both products are commonly available in hardware and paint stores.

Protecting Outside Faucets

Water that remains in an outside faucet may freeze during the winter and crack the supply pipe or faucet. To avoid this, trace the supply pipe of the outside faucet and find the cutoff valve. Usually it will be two to three feet behind the faucet in the basement. Close the

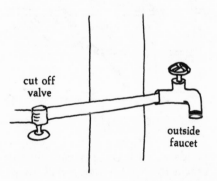

cut off valve

outside faucet

cutoff valve and open the outside faucet. This will drain the faucet and protect it and the pipe all winter.

Frozen Padlocks

Ice or snow that accumulates on a padlock can seep into the lock and cause freezing and subsequent rusting. It is, therefore, a good idea to keep ice and snow from getting

to a padlock by placing a leather cover over it, and keeping a piece of tape over the keyhole.

Strengthening a Leader Elbow

The aluminum elbow or nozzle at the bottom of a drainpipe leader often gets loose and falls off. The elbow helps divert water away from the foundation of the house. An easy way to keep it from falling off is to drill a hole through both elbow and leader and to insert an aluminum screw just slightly smaller in diameter than the hole drilled. Another solution is to drill a hole through the leader and elbow and to force in a long aluminum nail or a wood dowel.

Sliding Heavy Objects on Garage and Cellar Floors

Heavy crates can be slid easily across rough-surfaced floors and driveways when metal bottle caps are placed under the corners of the crates.

The caps can similarly be used for moving heavy furniture. If there's a chance that the edges of the cap will mark the furniture, line the caps with cloth or paper towelling. For furniture with large legs, large metal jar caps can be used.

Even indoors, the metal caps can be used without marking waxed floors, if an old sheet is placed over the area where the crate will slide.

Screening Damp Sand

A length of chain placed on the sifting screen before pouring on the sand will break up damp or lumpy sand and push it through the screen as you move the chain around.

Curing Concrete

Newly poured concrete must be cured—which means that it should be kept moist for four to five days. The thinner the cement slab that has been poured, the more the curing that is required. The periodic sprinkling of water on the concrete will prevent the moisture in the mixture from evaporating, and, consequently, prevent shrinkage and cracking.

Reinforcing Concrete

To reinforce cement, throw in any kind of scrap iron, including nails, chain links, etc., that is free of scaling, rust, oil, grease and dirt.

This reinforcement will help prevent the concrete from cracking, and will add strength to the slab by tying it together as one unit.

Vapor Barriers

New concrete floors to be poured for garage floors, basements, or fireplace bases can be protected against the passage of water vapor from the ground below by covering the area where the concrete will be poured with a sheet of polyethylene, four to six mils thick.

Patching Exterior Walls

If outside walls are covered with stucco, brick or other masonry, check in early fall for cracks or open joints that will allow moisture to enter. In very cold weather the water that enters the cracks ex-

pands when it freezes, causing the cracks to open further. Small cracks can be filled with caulking compound; larges ones should be filled with vinyl-concrete patching cement. Defective mortar joints in brick or cement block walls should be filled with freshly-mixed mortar cement. Before filling the cracks, scrape out about ½ to one inch of the old mortar.

Foundation Cracks

Large cracks in the foundation of a house are a sign of serious trouble and should be attended to. Call in a competent building contractor or consultant to look over the foundation as soon as you notice such cracks.

Holes in Concrete

Holes can be drilled in concrete by using two inexpensive tools available in most hardware stores: One is a star drill and the other a hand-drilling hammer. The star drill is about 18-inches long and has four sharp hardened steel vanes at one end. The hammer has a two-pound head and a short wooden handle. Each time you strike the end of the drill with the hammer you give it a quarter turn. Surprisingly, you can achieve just as much speed with these two tools as you can with an electric drill that has a carbide bit.

Coating a House

How many coats of paint does the exterior of a new house need? Two would be the usual answer. But it's the third coat that adds years of wear to the bare wood of a new house.

When to Repaint

If you're thinking of repainting a house more frequently than once every four years, that's probably too often. The outer coat will wear at the rate of about 1/1000 of an inch yearly. When a house is painted too often the outer coat becomes so thick it peels and cracks. Be sure your house needs a new coat of paint before doing the job. Very often you can give the exterior of your house a clean, fresh look by simply washing it down with water and a good cleaning agent that your hardware dealer can suggest.

When Not to Paint

There are times when it's best not to paint a house. Do not start a painting job during or soon after a rain when the wood is still wet. Also do not paint when the temperature is lower than 50 degrees Fahrenheit.

Exterior Paint Brushes

Buy the best paint brushes you can for painting a house. Better brushes hold more paint, lay the paint down better and last longer. Professional painters still consider animal-hair brushes the best.

A Season for Painting

The best time to paint is in the spring and fall when there are fewer insects. Allow three to five days for paint to dry between coats. Two coats are recommended when repainting.

The Price of Paint

Bargain prices in house paints do not exist very often. Better paints cost more because their ingredients cost more, and when you use good paint you will not need to repaint as often.

Part Two

Grounds
and Gardens

●━━●━━●━━●━━●━━●━━●━━●━━●━━●━━●━━●━━●━━●━━●━━●

Holes in Driveways

In order to patch large holes in driveways, clean out the hole and fill the bottom with clean, good-sized (3/4-inch) stones. Cover with stone and tar mix or cement, depending on the surface. Pre-mixed cement and sand can be purchased for such patching jobs.

Patching Blacktop Driveways

Blacktop driveways develop holes as a result of weathering and the oil drippings from cars. Before patching, the oil should be removed with trisodium phosphate (TSP), which can be purchased at a hardware store. It should be mixed with water according to directions on the package. Remove the TSP by flushing the driveway with water.

Patch holes and cracks with a mix of sand or fine gravel and cold liquid asphalt, also available at hardware stores. Very fine cracks can be filled with liquid asphalt poured from a small can. Allow 24 hours without traffic for the asphalt to harden.

Resurfacing Blacktop Driveways

Blacktop driveways that have been patched and freed of oil and grease can be resurfaced with cold, liquid asphalt or a special black vinyl latex paint. Both are heavy liquids that usually come in five-gallon cans. Pour out a gallon at a time on the driveway and smooth it with an old push-broom. The vinyl paint is slightly thinner than the liquid asphalt and is unaffected by oil, which dissolves asphalt, but it must be renewed each year.

Lawn Weeding

The best time to weed a lawn is in early spring. Waiting until later, when the weeds have flowered and seeded, will only make your job more difficult.

Chemical Weed Killers

Be wary of using chemical weed killers for lawns on which children and pets play. Many chemicals are toxic.

Reducing Lawn Erosion

Place a large flat stone under the drainspout. The rainwater will spread out over a wider area and keep topsoil from washing away.

Watering Helper

When you want to water flowers and shrubs located in a specific area, but do not want to stand and hold the hose, a coat hanger can be fashioned into a support for the hose, and the water can be directed as desired.

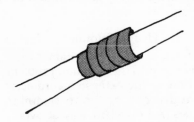

Repairing a Garden Hose

A small hole or crack in a rubber garden hose can be repaired with a rubber patch and some adhesive tape. Sand the surface around the hole lightly with fine sandpaper. Also sand the surface of the rubber patch which you can cut from an old tube. Apply contact cement to both sanded surfaces and wait until the cement is dry to the touch. Press the patch over the hole very firmly. Wrap the patched area with vinyl electrical or rubber tape.

Low cost Patios

When building a patio, it is the price of concrete that makes the cost so high. To reduce your cost use two-inch thick slats for the foundation, and flat stones for the surface. If you want a continuous surface, cement the stones at their edges. For a really level surface, you'll need to reset and recement the stones every several years. By using the slats, rather than concrete, for the foundation you'll save nearly 90% of the cost of a concrete base.

Broiling Over Charcoal

When broiling outdoors, it is important to start with a heaping pile of charcoal in order to end up with a large bed of burning coals. After the flames have died down, allow sufficient time for most of the charcoal to turn white before placing your meat on the grill. Trim away excess fat and keep the grill far enough from the coals so that the flames that shoot up periodically from the dripping fat do not burn the meat. The best outdoor broiling results are gotten with steaks and hamburgers. It is wise, at the outset, to turn meat over about 30 seconds after first placing it on the grill so that both sides are seared. This will save most of the juices from being wasted.

Reusing Charcoal

Charcoal broiling can be rather expensive, but one way to cut the cost is to put the fire out as soon as you're finished cooking. Douse the coals with a pot of water, allow to dry, and use the charcoal again. Alternately, the charcoal can be placed in a metal pan with a tight-fitting lid. When the lid goes on, the fire goes out.

Beach Umbrellas

You can lengthen the life of your beach umbrella or an awning if you open it up after a rain to allow the air to dry it out. Material not exposed to air and daylight will mildew and rot. The same applies to lawn chairs with fabric seats.

Renewing Umbrellas and Awnings

Canvas outdoor umbrellas and faded awnings can be given a new lease on life with a fresh coat of paint. Use canvas paint and a wide brush. Take quick, even strokes to avoid streaks.

Pitted Aluminum Furniture

Remove the black pock-marks from aluminum by rubbing firmly with fine steel wool. Apply a thin coat of paste wax and polish well. Allow 20 minutes for drying before buffing. Waxing once or twice a year thereafter will prevent subsequent pitting. Between waxings, wash the aluminum monthly with mild detergent to keep it fresh looking.

Pipe Legs

To make a table that can be quickly dismantled and transported (e.g. for picnics), use ordinary pipe threaded at one end for the legs. Attach a standard pipe flange under the table top, and screw the pipe into the flange. To protect finished floors, slide rubber crutch tips over the bottom ends of the pipes. You can buy the tips, the pipe and the flange at your hardware store.

Snow Shovels

To keep snow from sticking to your snow shovel, spray it with a silicone lubricant. Silicone, like wax, repels water. It is also a good idea to spray some on your skis, ice skates and rubbers to prevent snow from adhering.

Outdoor Furniture

Red cedar and redwood are naturally resistant to decay. Red cedar is commonly used for house shingles and clapboards. If you are going to make outdoor wooden furniture or bird feeders, use redwood. A pigmented stain is all the finish you need for furniture. Bird houses or feeders can be left unfinished and will turn a silvery gray without decaying.

Hedge Trimmers

If you use a hedge trimmer, you may run into the common problem of finding the extension cord accidentally cut by your trimmer blades. An excellent way of avoiding this is to slit a three-to-five-foot section of old garden hose down the center, spread it apart, and let it wrap itself around the electric wire cord. Wind some electrical tape around both ends of the garden hose and continue to wind it until it is secure. The thick garden hose

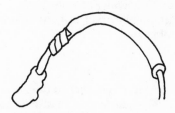

Testing Seeds

Before sowing last year's seed—or the seed from the year before—make sure it will produce. Place a few seeds between two damp sheets of paper towel. Keep them in a warm area for five to ten days. If 75% of the seeds send out sprouts, the seeds will produce when planted.

Transferring Seedlings Outdoors

When the soil is warm enough, young plants started indoors should be transferred outdoors. Dig a hole in the soil for each peat pot, large enough so that each pot rests ½-inch below the level of the ground. Fill each hole with water and allow it to drain. Put each peat pot in a hole and fill in around the pot with earth pressed firmly around the pot and base of the plant. Then add a liquid fertilizer.

A Child's Garden

Even if it's only a row or two, set aside a portion of the vegetable or flower garden for your young children to plant some seeds. Let them do some of the spading and raking in preparation for planting, and have them do some of the weeding and watering of their rows.

will prevent the trimmer's teeth from cutting the electrical wire.

Losing Garden Tools

Garden tools left on the lawn are often hard to find because their coloring is so close to that of the landscape. To save the time and energy the search takes, dip the handles of your garden tools into yellow or orange enamel outdoor paint. The coating will last for years and your tools will always be easy to locate if lost on the lawn or in the brush.

Protecting Garden Tools

During a long winter of disuse, moisture is apt to attack unprotected garden tools, encrusting them with rust. To avoid wasting the time you would have to spend removing the winter rust, spray oil over your rakes, shovels and pruning shears before you put them away in the fall. After spraying with oil, you can protect them further by wrapping each with rags or newspapers.

Seed Potency

Seeds lose their vitality with age, and most of the more commonly used vegetable seeds are good for only one to three years.

Sagging Garden Gates

To correct your sagging garden gate, what you need is a turnbuckle. Buy a buckle and rod set that will fit the gate. Or, buy only the buckle and use two turns of heavy galvanized wire for the rod. The buckle will raise up the side with the hinges to the level of the lower side (the swinging side).

Transplanting Trees

The best time to transplant trees is in the late fall or early spring. The ground is then still workable, and the tree is dormant. In fall, transplant after the first, hard frost, and in spring before the buds begin to swell. Most roots will grow at temperatures above 45 degrees Fahrenheit, so if you are able to transplant right after the first hard fall frost, or several weeks before the buds emerge in spring, the tree will have time to establish its root system.

Unwanted Animals

Dogs and other unwanted animals can be kept out of flower and shrub beds by sprinkling moth balls over the area.

Garden Kneeler

For more comfortable kneeling while doing garden chores, stuff old nylon stockings in a hot water bottle. You will not only have an instant kneeling pad, but one that is washable too!

Nail Dirt

It's easier to get dirt under your nails while gardening than it is to get it out. Avoid the problem by scratching your nails against a bar of soap before beginning garden work.

Making a Garden Walk

Use flat stepping stones to create your own garden walk. Stepping stones need not have a cement base. Slates, at least two inches thick, can be substituted for the concrete bases. Allow the grass to grow in around them, and the slates will stay in place.

Felling Trees

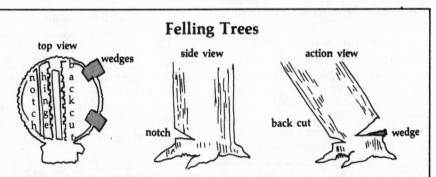

Before cutting down a tree, consider the wind direction, the natural lean of the tree, and whether the trunk is sound, hollow or partially rotted. Watch for dead limbs overhead. Then, cut a notch 1/3 the diameter of the trunk in the direction of the line of fall. Make the back cut at least two inches higher than the notch, leaving a hinge of uncut wood to guide the tree over. If there is a chance that the tree might not fall in the desired direction, use wedges to open the back cut and tilt the tree in the desired direction of fall. Never let a wedge come into contact with a vibrating chainsaw because the wedge will kick back.

Chapter Eight

MONEY
AND
ENERGY
SAVING
HINTS

Part One

Plumbing and Heating

To Speed-up Slow Flowing Faucets

If the water from your faucet flows out slowly, you probably have a clogged aerator. The aerator is screwed to the end of the faucet and consists of two or more round screens. These screens filter out the dirt or sediment that may be in the water supply. When the fine openings of the screen are clogged, the water does not come through evenly, and the flow is straggly or feeble.

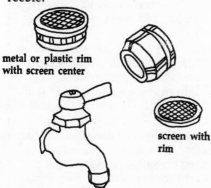

metal or plastic rim with screen center

screen with rim

To correct the problem, remove the aerator and clean away the trapped particles. Be sure to re-member the order in which you removed the round screens so you can replace them exactly as they were.

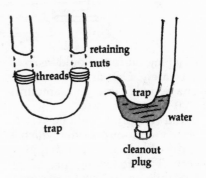

Clean-out Plugs

Most sinks have a clean-out plug at the bottom of the U-shaped tubing under the sink. Place a pan under the plug, unscrew it, and with a piece of wire (from a coat hanger) clear the trap of accumulated material. Then screw the plug back into position.

169

Repairing a Leaky Faucet

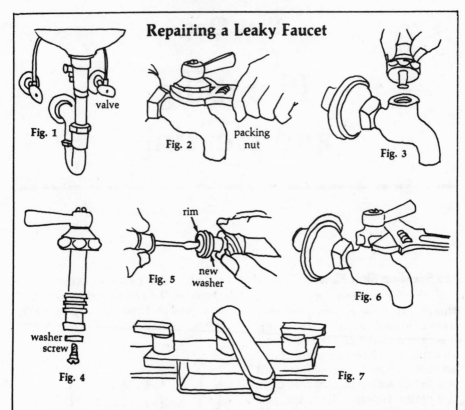

Fig. 1 valve

Fig. 2 packing nut

Fig. 3

Fig. 4 washer screw

Fig. 5 rim new washer

Fig. 6

Fig. 7

Dripping faucets should be fixed immediately. One drip per second, over a period of one year, amounts to 700 gallons of water.

If you try, you should be able to replace a worn-out washer which is usually the cause of a dripping faucet. The following procedure can be followed in most situations:

1. Turn off the water at the shut-off valve nearest to the faucet you are going to repair, and then open the faucet until the water stops flowing. (Fig. 1)
2. Loosen the packing nut with a wrench. (Fig. 2) (Most nuts loosen by turning counterclockwise.) Pull out the valve unit. (Fig. 3)
3. Remove the screw holding the old washer at the bottom of the valve unit. (Fig. 4)
4. Put in new washer that fits snugly, and replace screw. (Fig. 5)
5. Put valve unit back in faucet with handle in the same position as when you removed it.
6. Tighten the packing nut. (Fig. 6)
7. Turn on the water at the shut-off valve. Faucets may look different, but they are all about the same. Mixing faucets, which are used on sinks, laundry tubs, and bathtubs are actually two separate units with the same spout. You'll need to repair each unit separately. (Fig. 7)

Clogged Sinks I

When the sink is clogged and the water drains out slowly, you may have to remove the U-shaped pipe

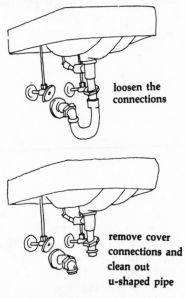

loosen the connections

remove cover connections and clean out u-shaped pipe

under the sink, unless Drano or a similar product will unclog it. The pipes under the sink are rounded in order to hold some water that will trap odors from septic tank or sewer line. In addition, it traps bobby pins, rings, and numerous other objects that can clog a sink. Remove the U-shaped pipe by loosening the connecting nuts, and clean it out. If this does not clear the drain, buy a snake at a hardware store and probe deeply into the pipe to loosen the clogged material.

Clogged Sinks II

If you have used a plunger, but your sink is still clogged, the best tool to use for cleaning out plumbing is a "snake." This tool is a tightly wound, very flexible hollow cable

which comes in lengths of 10 to 35 feet (and more). It has a handle that permits the unit to rotate as it is turned and pushed back and forth in the clogged pipe. The handle can move up or down the snake to give the user as much length as is needed. A setscrew in the side of the handle can be tightened to hold the handle at any desired point along the length of the snake. Both hands are used to turn the handle. In most cases the snake will clear a clogged pipe.

Drain Stoppers

If your sink is clogged and it is necessary to remove the stopper in order to use a snake or a plunger, the linkage of the stopper, which is beneath the sink, must be removed. Loosen the thumbscrew that holds the upper and lower rods together. Pull the upper rod out through the top of the sink. This will free the lower rod and permit you to pull

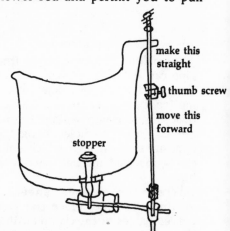

make this straight

thumb screw

move this forward

stopper

out the horizontal rod that goes into the bottom of the stopper. Take out the stopper and use the plunger or snake.

Pipe Condensation

Cold water pipes often sweat during warm weather, and the wetness may leave stains on the floor and cause mildew. Insulation is the simplest way to control condensation. If the pipe insulation available seems too expensive, buy some ¼-inch sponge rubber self-sticking weatherstripping which comes packaged in coils, and is inexpensive. Remove the protective paper from the adhesive and apply the stripping in a tightly wound spiral until the pipe is covered. Be sure the pipe is dry before applying the insulation or weatherstripping.

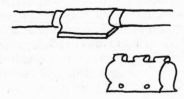

Leaking Pipes I

A small hole in a copper or iron pipe can be repaired with a pipe clamp and a piece of rubber sheeting from an inner tube or garden hose. A pipe clamp is hinged along one side and has holes along the opposite side through which bolts can be inserted and tightened with nuts.

Wrap the rubber sheeting around the pipe, place the two curved halves of the clamp around the rubber and secure it in place with nuts and bolts. If holes develop on either side of the patch at a later date, it is best to replace the entire length of pipe.

Leaking Pipes II

Leaks that occur where pipes are joined at tees, elbows and similar places can often be fixed with epoxy putty. Epoxy is a powerful, waterproof adhesive that sets very hard. In putty form it comes in two sticks of identical size and shape.

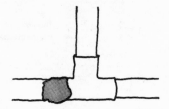

Cut equal pieces from each stick, press them together and work them into each other for several minutes until the dough is uniform. Turn the water in the pipe off and apply the putty to the joint. Wait 24 hours before turning the water on again.

Frozen Pipes

Too much sudden heat can cause frozen pipes to burst because ice in the pipes may expand. To thaw frozen pipes, do so slowly. Dip rags in hot water, and wrap them around the pipes. When the rags lose their heat, repeat the process.

Radiator Heat

Much radiator heat warms up the wall rather than the room. Aluminum foil placed behind radiators will reflect more heat back into the room.

Conserving Room Energy

Even if your home is adequately insulated, caulked, and weatherstripped, you can save additional energy:

1. Make sure radiator covers do not restrict the flow of heat. At least 75% of the surface of a radiator cover should have grille openings so as to allow for free heat flow.
2. Cover your floors with rugs or carpets. They offer much more insulation than tile, linoleum, wood or slate. The thicker the carpet, the greater the insulation value. Wool and acrylic fibers provide the best insulation.
3. Position your furniture far enough away from radiators and vents to permit free circulation of heated or cooled air.

Sealing Rooms

Closing off rooms that are seldom used will cut heating or air conditioning costs. The door should be well-sealed against air passing over the threshold. If there's space for air to pass, add weatherstripping.

Window Shade Insulation

Pulling the shades at night not only gives you privacy, it also saves fuel costs. The shades partially insulate the windows. They keep out the heat in summer, and the cold in winter.

Storm Windows

Let your storm windows keep your electric bills down in the summer as they do in the winter. If your house has central air conditioning or if you have room air conditioners, keep the lower glass of the storm window in the same position

during the summer as well as in winter. The cool air generated by your air conditioner will not be dissipated as quickly.

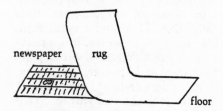

For Warmer Floors

Before laying a carpet or throw rug, place a layer of newspaper directly on the floor or over the padding on the floor. The newspaper will insulate the rug.

Furnace Check-up

You will save money and conserve energy if you will call in a serviceman to clean your furnace every summer. Don't do it yourself. It should be done by experienced people. It is even worthwhile to sign a service contract with your oil supplier. Annual furnace clean-up is part of the deal.

Hot Furnaces

If your basement is too hot, check the furnace. Browned areas near the warm-air ducts or scorched areas above the heater are a message being sent to you. They are saying that it is time to call in an expert to check over the heating unit.

Black Smoke

Black smoke coming out of a chimney is an indication that it's time to call in a serviceman.

Air Ducts

If your warm air heating system has a loose joint in one of the ducts through which warm air is escaping, you can repair it with a special tape made for the purpose. It is called Duct Tape, and is available in many hardware stores. It is a heat-resistant cloth material with a plastic coating and a powerful adhesive. Remove dust and dirt from the duct with detergent and water. Strip protective paper from the adhesive and press the tape against the loose joint.

Gas Pipe Leak

To determine the location of a leak in a gas pipe, spread thick suds along the section of the pipe where the leak is suspected. If there is a leak at that point, the escaping gas

will cause the suds to bubble right at that spot.

Main Gas Valve

Be prepared for an emergency, and learn how to shut off the main gas valve. It is located near the gas meter in your cellar or utility room. Usually the shut-off valve is on a pipe leading to or from the meter. The valve that controls the meter is usually a square flat metal tab with a hole in it. The valve is open when the metal tab is in line with the pipe. It is closed when the tab is projecting at right angles to the pipe. You cannot release the valve with your fingers so take a wrench along when you go looking for it.

Part Two

Electricity
and Electrical Wiring

Three-Way Bulb Adaptors

Any table lamp can be adapted to the larger socket-size required for the use of 3-way bulbs of the 30-70-100 or 50-100-150 varieties. A simple adaptor, which screws into the standard socket, is available at most hardware or electrical supply stores.

Wall Switches

Small appliances that do not have their own on-off switches can be operated more conveniently by using plug-in wall switches. The advantage is that you don't have to

pull out or push in the plug to turn the appliance off or on.

Combination Outlet

If you have only one ceiling light fixture in your garage or cellar but need a power outlet, there are two adaptors which can provide it for you. One is a Y-shaped double

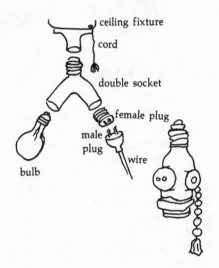

socket and the other is a pull-chain current tap with two convenient outlets. Both will provide light and power at one time.

Repairing Electric Plugs

Fig. 1	Fig. 2	Fig. 3	Fig. 4	Fig. 5

Fig. 6	Fig. 7	Fig. 8

Fig. 9	Fig. 10	Fig. 11

If your lamp or appliance does not work, your problem may be a defective plug. A prong may be loose or broken, or the cord may be damaged in some manner. To play safe, replace your two-prong plug. This is how to do it:

1. Cut the cord off at the damaged part. (Fig. 1)
2. Slip the plug back on the cord. (Fig. 2)
3. Clip and separate the cord. (Fig. 3)
4. Tie knot. (Fig. 4)
5. Remove a half-inch of the insulation from the end of the wires. (Fig. 5)
6. Twist small wires together, clockwise. (Fig. 6)
7. Pull knot down firmly in the plug. (Fig. 7)
8. Pull one wire around each terminal to the screw. (Fig. 8)
9. Wrap the wire around the screw, clockwise. (Fig. 9)
10. Tighten the screw. Insulation should come to the screw but not under it. (Fig. 10).
11. Place insulation cover back over the plug. (Fig. 11)

Time-delay Switches

A time-delay switch will give you the time necessary to switch off the light and leave the area while the light is still shining. It is extremely valuable for safety reasons, and installing it is not difficult. Follow the same procedure as when replacing a wall switch.

Splicing Wires

To join two electric wires, trim insulation about 3/4 of an inch from ends of both wires. If the wire is soft and consists of many fine filaments, twist the filaments tightly together, then scrape with a sharp knife until the copper is clean and shiny. Twist both wires together in

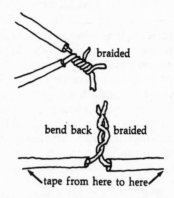

a tight braid and bend the unit back till it lies flat against the insulation of one of the wires. Then, wrap the area in tape, extending the tape from one inch below the joined wires to one inch above them.

Male Plug Wiring

To connect the wires from a lamp or small appliance to a male plug, strip the insulation for about 3/4 of an inch from the end of each wire. Insert the cord through the plug and tie the two wires in the "Underwriter's Knot" as shown in the drawing. The knot will prevent the wires from being pulled loose if you accidentally remove the plug by

pulling the cord instead of grasping the plug. Bend the bare ends of the wires into the shape of hooks, pull the insulated part of the wire around the base of each prong as shown, and place the bare hook around the terminal screw. Tighten the screw with screwdriver and replace fiber cover. (See illustration.)

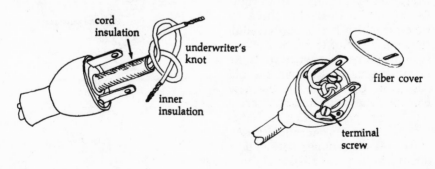

Frayed Insulation

Lamps sometimes fail to work because of a break in the wire of the lamp cord, and it is usually easier to repair the break than to rewire the lamp. The two adjoining wires of most lamp cords are easily separated with a sharp knife or razor. Wrap vinyl electric tape around the individual wire with the broken insulation, then bring both wires together and wrap the unit with more tape. Use vinyl electric tape.

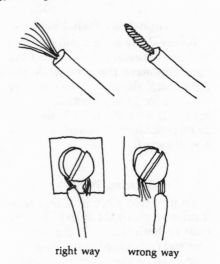

right way   wrong way

Fastening Electrical Wires

There's a correct way to fasten an electrical wire under a lug (screw). First strip away about 1/2 inch of the insulation, baring the wire, then twist the end strands of the wire so that they become like one piece. Wrap the wire around the screw in a clockwise direction and tighten the screw with a screwdriver in a clockwise direction.

Replacing a Lamp Socket

When a socket switch fails, the entire socket must be replaced. To do so, first remove the plug from the wall outlet. Then, to remove the worn out part, loosen the little setscrew at the base of the socket with a screwdriver. Unscrew the old socket by turning it from right to left until it clears the threaded tube on which it is mounted. Pull the upper part of the socket off its core, and loosen the wires from the terminal screws. Remove the old base from the wires, slip the new base over the wires, and then screw it down on the mounting tube. Attach wires to new terminal screw and press new upper socket part down firmly on new base. Tighten setscrew against the new base.

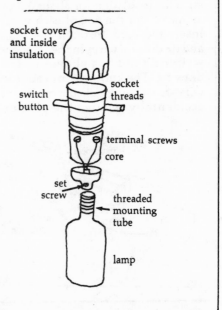

socket cover and inside insulation

switch button

socket threads

terminal screws

core

set screw

threaded mounting tube

lamp

Fluorescent White

There are three types of fluorescent white: daylight, cool white, and warm white. Daylight is used primarily for display lighting, especially for store windows. Cool white blends well with natural light and is used in schools, factories and offices. Warm white is the most efficient, but highlights orange, yellow and yellow-green at the expense of other colors, which makes its light warmer and more pleasant, and is why it is the choice of most homeowners.

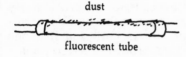

dust

fluorescent tube

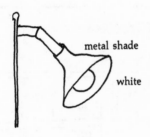

metal shade

white

Loss of Light

Accumulations of dust on incandescent light bulbs and fluorescent tubes greatly reduces their light. Make sure power is off, and then use a damp cloth to remove the dust. Dust or dirt on the white finish of metal reflectors and lamp shades also causes unnecessary loss of light. It can usually be removed with water and mild detergent or ammonia.

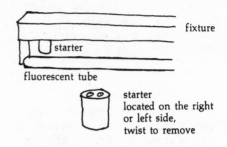

fixture

starter

fluorescent tube

starter
located on the right
or left side,
twist to remove

Fluorescent Lamp Life

Don't turn fluorescent lights on and off frequently as this shortens their life. Fluorescents work best in temperatures not lower than 50 degrees Fahrenheit. When replacing the starter be sure you purchased the right kind. Check the number on the old starter against the number on the replacement. Flickering bulbs are often the result of defective starters.

Worn-out Fluorescents

As they age, fluorescent tubes shed less and less light. The change is usually so gradual that most people are not aware of the loss of light. A good indication that it is time to replace the tube is when it becomes dark at both ends. If the light flickers unevenly or doesn't seem to reach full brightness, al-

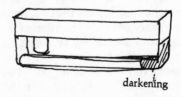

darkening

though the ends of the tube have not darkened, it is the starter, not the tube, that should be replaced.

Dark Tubes

A fluorescent tube that darkens need not necessarily be replaced. Reversing the tube, sometimes, will brighten it at the dark end.

Identifying Fuses

If you want to determine which fuse or circuit breaker controls a particular outlet, plug a radio into the outlet in question, and turn it up to a high volume. Then, unscrew the various fuses in succession. When the radio has stopped playing, you will know that you have just cut off the fuse that controls the outlet into which the radio was plugged. Mark the fuse accordingly. If your house has circuit breakers, rather than fuses, the procedure is the same.

Radio & TV Interference

Your radio or TV set is not necessarily in need of repair if, at times, the sound is muffled or the picture is distorted. Interference may be due to an airplane passing overhead or to adverse weather conditions. But there are times when the cause of the problem is right in your own house. If the radio or TV is plugged into an outlet on the same line as a fluorescent light fixture, you may experience bad reception. The next time you have bad reception, observe what happens when you turn off the fluorescent fixture. If the fluorescent fixture proves to have been the cause of the problem, try plugging your radio or TV into different outlets until you find one that gives trouble-free reception.

Overloaded Circuits

Too many lights and appliances on a single circuit will blow a fuse or flip a circuit breaker to the off position, shutting off all current on that circuit. To test for an overloaded circuit, unplug all the lamps and appliances on that circuit, then insert a working fuse or circuit breaker to "on." Plug in one appliance at a time so that it is the only one using that circuit. If you reach a point where the fuse blows, that particular appliance probably has defective wiring, and should be repaired. If there is nothing wrong with the appliance (try it in another outlet to find out), then you may be sure the fuse blew because you are overloading the circuit.

cover

circuit breaker off

Part Three

Electrical Appliances

Instruction Manuals

Whenever you buy a new appliance—a refrigerator, a stove, toaster or drill—always read the instruction sheet or manual carefully, and be sure to *save* it. There will likely be many occasions when you will have a question about the operation of the appliance. In most cases, the answer will be there, right in the manual.

Labeling Appliances

It is a good idea to keep the label on appliances that you acquire. The information on the label may prove valuable at a later date. To keep that information legible, coat the label with shellac right after buying the appliance. This applies also to electric tools. The information on the label will save you time, money and effort when you call for service or must replace a part.

Efficient Lighting

It is more economical to use one large bulb than several small ones. A 100-watt bulb gives as much light as six 25-watt bulbs, but only uses about two-thirds as much current.

Television Lighting

Watching television in a darkened room is tiring to the eyes because of the contrast between the bright screen and dark surroundings. To avoid eyestrain, make sure there is some light in the viewing area. Portable lamps placed behind or at the sides of the set will prevent reflections on the TV screen.

Table Lamps

Before you shop for table lamps, jot down the heights of tables on which lamps will be placed, and the height of any chair or sofa seat on which a person using the lamp will be seated. Take these figures with you as you shop. You may also want to consider the eye level height of persons using a lamp, particularly if an individual is unusually tall or short. Keep this rule in mind: Table height plus lamp base height (to the lower edge of shade) should equal the eye height of the person using the lamp.

Lighting Maintenance

Home lighting equipment needs regular care and cleaning. Dirt and dust on bulbs, tubes, diffusion bowls, lampshades, and fixtures can cause a substantial loss in light output. Clean all lighting equipment at least four times a year—bowl-type portable lamps should be cleaned monthly.

Here are some suggestions for taking care of lamps and electrical parts:

1. Wash glass and plastic diffusers and shields in a detergent solution, rinse in clear warm water, and dry.
2. Wipe bulbs and tubes with a damp, soapy cloth, and dry well.
3. Dust wood and metal lamp bases with a soft cloth and apply a thin coat of wax. Glass, pottery, marble, chrome, and onyx bases can be washed with a damp soapy cloth, dried, and waxed.
4. Lampshades may be cleaned by a vacuum cleaner with a soft brush attachment, or dry-cleaned. Silk or rayon shades that are hand sewn to the frame, with no glued trimmings, may be washed in mild, lukewarm suds, and rinsed in clear water. Dry shades quickly to prevent rusting of frames.
5. Wipe parchment shades with a dry cloth.
6. Remove plastic wrappings from lampshades before using. Wrappings create glare and may warp the frame and wrinkle the shade fabric. Some are fire hazards.
7. Replace all darkened bulbs. A darkened bulb can reduce light output 25 to 50 percent, but uses almost the same amount of current as a new bulb operating at correct wattage. Darkened bulbs may be used in closets or hallways where less light is needed.
8. Replace fluorescent tubes that flicker and any tubes that have darkened ends. A long delay in starting indicates a new starter is probably needed. If a humming sound develops in a fluorescent fixture, the ballast may need to be remounted or replaced.

Dimmer Controls

Add flexibility to your home lighting by using dimmer controls on fixtures in bedrooms, bathrooms, halls, and living rooms. Gradations of light, from full bright to very dim, are possible simply by turning a knob. A low level of lighting is helpful in the care of small children, sick persons, and others who need assistance during the night.

You can make dramatic changes in the mood of a room by softening lights with a dimmer switch. Lights can be lowered when listening to music or enjoying a fire on the hearth.

Dimmer-switch controlled lamps give greater flexibility than three-way lamps that use three-way sockets and require three-way bulbs.

Three-way Sockets

Three-way bulbs have three fila-ments and require three-way sock-ets. Each filament can be operated separately or in combination. Make sure that a three-way bulb is tight-ened in the socket so both contacts in the screw-in base are touching firmly.

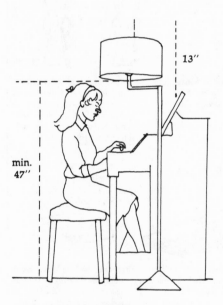

Piano Lamp

To read music and play the piano, center the shade of a swing-arm floor lamp 22 inches to the right or left of the middle of the keyboard, and 13 inches in front of the lower edge of music rack.

High-intensity Lamps

The small high-intensity lamps now on the market are not de-signed for study, reading, or gener-al work. They can, however, provide a concentrated area of high-level light for special tasks, such as sewing, crafts, or fine-de-tail work. They should always be used in combination with good gen-eral lighting.

Reading Lamps

For reading, a floor lamp with a fixed or swing-arm is correctly placed when the light comes from behind the shoulder of the reader, near the rear of the chair, either at the right or the left, but never from directly behind the chair.

Floor Lamps

In choosing a floor lamp, keep in mind exactly where it is to be lo-cated in your home. Choose lamps sized and constructed for proper placement without interfering with house traffic. Small floor lamps, standard, swing-arm, or bridge type, may be 43 to 47 inches from the floor to the bottom of the shade. Large lamps, standard or swing-arm, measure 45 to 49 inches from the floor to the bottom of the shade.

Bare Bulbs

Cover all bare bulbs or tubes in a ceiling fixture with a shade or dif-fuser. Some of these diffusers clip to the bulb. Others hang from small chains attached to the husk of the fixture. Large diffusers, some-times called adaptors, may have supporting frames that are screwed on the sockets of single-bulb fix-tures. An inexpensive way to avoid the glare of bare bulbs in a ceiling fixture is to replace these bulbs with silver bowl bulbs or decorative mushroom-shaped bulbs.

Types of Lighting Fixtures

BATHROOM

Side and overhead fluorescent fixtures. Pair of 24-inch long fixtures are spaced 30 or more inches apart at mirror sides. Use fixture above mirror if no ceiling light in room.

Vapor-proof ceiling fixture. A good type for a shower stall. Use a 60-watt bulb Make sure that the switch is located outside of the shower.

Side and overhead incandescent units. One- or two-socket fixtures at mirror sides are centered 60 inches above floor. Note overhead fixture. Bulbs are well shielded to reduce glare.

UTILITY ROOM

Surface-mounted ceiling fixture. Minimum diameter of 12 inches is desirable. Unit may have one or two sockets.

Shielded fluorescent fixture. Two- or four-tube fixture can be centered in ceiling or mounted over work area.

Reflector and reflector bowl bulb unit. Twelve- or 14-inch minimum diameter. Use to reduce glare and to spread light.

HALLWAY

Hanging bowl fixture. Eight-inch diameter. A good choice for lighting a high-ceilinged hall or stairway.

Closed globe fixture. Unit is mounted on ceiling. Choose a white glass globe for diffusion of light.

Wall bracket fixture. May be used to supplement general lighting. Can be mounted on wall near a mirror.

Types of Lighting Fixtures

KITCHEN

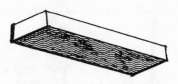

Closed globe unit. Minimum diameter of bowl is 14 inches. White glass gives good diffusion of light.

Shielded fixture. Three or four sockets, 14 to 17-inch diameter. Shallow-wide bowl is desirable.

Fluorescent fixture with diffusing shield. Two or four tubes as needed in a 48-inch unit. For a large kitchen, two 2-tube fixtures can be placed end to end.

DINING ROOM

Lantern-style pulldown. Unit has a three-way socket, takes a 50/100/150-watt bulb, and a diffusing globe.

Ventilated ceiling fixture. Bent glass diffuser, 14-inch minimum diameter. Interior reflecting surfaces should be white or polished.

Pulldown fixture. Ventilated unit has three-way single socket or three sockets, and white glass diffuser.

BEDROOM

Surface mounted ceiling fixture. Twelve-inch minimum diameter, single socket or three sockets. Shallow-wide diffuser is desirable.

Ceiling fixture. Is similar to one on left. Twelve- or 14-inch width. Surface-mounted, with plain or textured glass or plastic diffuser.

Ventilated ceiling fixture. One or two sockets, diffusing shade to extend below trim to give side lighting. Unit is surface-mounted on ceiling.

Correct Placement for a Number of
Table and Floor Lamp Combinations

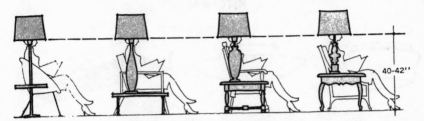

TYPICAL HEIGHTS OF LAMPS AND TABLES FOR SHADE AT EYE LEVEL

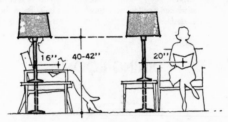

PLACEMENT DIMENSIONS FOR SHADE
AT EYE LEVEL

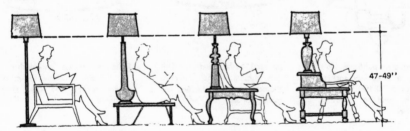

TYPICAL HEIGHTS OF LAMPS AND TABLES FOR SHADE ABOVE EYE LEVEL

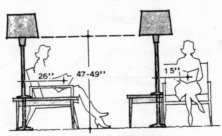

PLACEMENT DIMENSIONS FOR SHADE
ABOVE EYE LEVEL

Types of Diffusers

Undershade diffusers are now being offered by manufacturers for use in study and reading lamps. One is a highly reflective, inverted metal cone. Other new diffusers are bowl-shaped, prismatic reflectors. Shields prevent glare.

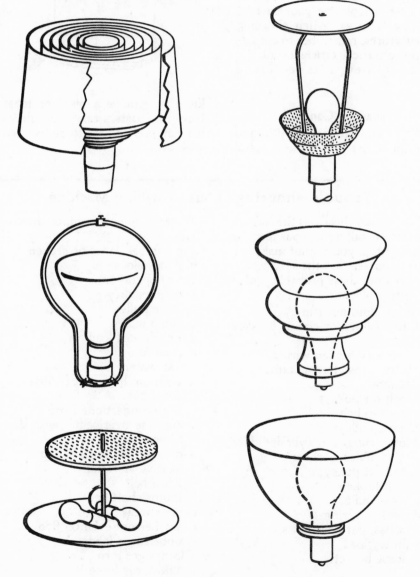

Types of Lighting Fixtures

The fixtures illustrated here for kitchen, dining room, and bedroom have design features that permit them to function more effectively in certain areas of the house. Use them as a guide when you are thinking of replacing your current lighting fixtures. When choosing new fixtures, remember to consider the electrical efficiency of the fixture as well as its decorative effect.

Toasters Can Kill

While your toaster is plugged into an outlet never use a metal knife to remove a piece of toast from it. Toasters carry considerable wattage, and are to be handled with caution.

Trouble-shooting Your Washing Machine

You should check out the following before calling a repairman. If you find that you cannot make the repair yourself, ask the serviceman to check out these probable causes of your problem.

1. Motor does not run
   a. fuse blown or circuit breaker off
   b. loose or broken wiring
2. Motor runs, but agitator does not move
   a. belt off pulleys
   b. broken belt
   c. loose pulleys
3. Motor runs, but cylinder does not (tumbler washers)
   a. belt off pulleys
   b. belt broken
   c. loose pulleys
   d. broken spring
4. Washes, but does not spin
   a. heavy load
   b. loose basket

5. Water does not drain, or drains slowly
   a. pump belt loose or broken
   b. pulleys loose
6. Noisy operation
   a. motor pulley
   b. drive pulley
   c. pump pulley
   d. unbalanced load
   e. cracked belt
7. Leaks water
   a. door or lid gasket loose or dried out
   b. hose connections loose
   c. machine overloaded with detergent
   d. door or lid out of alignment
8. Excessive vibration
   a. worn belt
   b. motor shaft bent
   c. floor weak
   d. washer not even on floor
   e. unbalanced load
9. Clothes get torn
   a. agitator is loose.

Trouble-shooting Your Vacuum

If your vacuum cleaner doesn't run at all or does not pick up dirt effectively, your problem may be one of the following. Check each out yourself before going to get service.

Tank (Cannister) Type

1. Is nozzle clogged?
2. Is there an obstruction in the hose?
3. Is the bag full?
4. Is the bag broken?
5. Is the filter old or clogged?
6. Is air leaking from the hose?

Upright Cleaner

1. Is nozzle clogged?
2. Does brush need cleaning?
3. Is there an obstruction in the bag?
4. Is the bag old?
5. Is the belt broken?
6. Is the belt weak or loose?

Dusting Light Bulbs—And Lamp Shades

It's a good idea to dust light bulbs when dusting other objects in the room. A dusty light bulb can produce 50% less light. A dusty lamp shade also cuts down on the amount of light projected.

Selecting Lamp Shades

Light, transparent lamp shades reflect more light than those of darker colors. The more light, the better you'll see and the cozier the room will look.

Trouble-shooting your TV

You might be able to check out the following before calling in your TV serviceman. If you cannot make the repair yourself, you can suggest one or more of these as a probable cause of the problem.

1. No picture or sound
   a. check if cord is connected
   b. check if plug is in outlet
   c. check fine tuning control
   d. check antenna connections
2. Weak or snowy picture
   a. check fine tuning control
   b. check antenna connection
   c. check contrast or brightness control
3. Picture too high or low
   a. adjust vertical height control (located in back of or under picture tube)
4. Bars in picture
   a. adjust horizontal and vertical controls.

Saving Money on Electricity

Once the habit is acquired, it's easy to turn off lights when you leave a room and turn them back on when you return. Bit by bit that reduction in the use of electricity will be reflected in your electric bill.

189

Chapter Nine

TIPS
ON
CAR
CARE

Gas Saving Tips

1. Turn off your engine if you stop more than a minute. Restarting uses less gasoline than a minute's idling.
2. Avoid pressing your accelerator all the way down when climbing hills and long grades. It wastes gasoline.
3. Jumpy starts and fast getaways will burn over 50 percent more gasoline than normal acceleration.
4. Check your tire pressure every month. Low tire pressure increases rolling resistance, causes increased tire wear, and reduces gasoline mileage.

The First Crucial Minutes

If you want to reduce fuel consumption, don't be in a hurry to make a fast getaway. Shift from low to second only after reaching 10 miles per hour, and from second to high only after 25 miles per hour. If your car has automatic drive, let the motor run a minute or two before you pull out into the street.

Fast Acceleration

Fast acceleration consumes unnecessary amounts of fuel. So does pumping the accelerator when you're waiting at a traffic light.

Engine Racing

Avoid racing a cold engine. Racing the engine burns a terrific amount of gas, and results in a lot of engine wear.

Speeding

High speed driving consumes a great deal of gas. Drive at moderate speeds to save on fuel costs. You will then not have to come to sudden stops, and you will conserve fuel and tire wear. Particularly, when you speed while negotiating curves you are decreasing the lifespan of your tire tenfold.

Air Filters

Much gasoline is wasted when you do not clean or change your air filter regularly. To burn less fuel, keep the air filter clean.

Engine Temperature

If the engine runs cold, a richer mixture of fuel will be required—and that will show up in fuel costs. Have the thermostat adjusted or replaced if the engine habitually runs cold.

Spark Plugs

Weak spark plugs can prevent complete combustion of the fuel. To avoid the accompanying higher consumption of fuel, have spark plugs, along with distributor points and battery ignition coil, checked regularly.

Carburetor Adjustment

There is no need to burn too rich a mixture of fuel. A carburetor that is not adjusted properly can provide too rich a mix. Twice a year, or every 5,000 miles, have the carburetor adjusted.

Cold Weather Starting

When starting up in cold weather, pump the accelerator a couple of times first to charge the intake system with fuel.

Tire Pressure

Keep your tires inflated to the pressure recommended in your driver's manual. Driving with less than the recommended pressure can reduce the amount of wear the tires will provide by as much as 25%. Too much or too little pressure makes for a much more uncomfortable ride.

Tire Checks

Small cuts and breaks in tires tend to grow deeper, and they invite the entry of dirt and water which, in time, destroy the cord structure. Check tires frequently for imbedded nails and glass.

Tire Longevity

Rotate your wheels two times a year to be sure of even wear. Include the spare in the rotation. When treads wear unevenly, a shimmy will develop, making for a very uncomfortable ride. Also, tires will last much longer if your brakes are well-adjusted, and if you avoid coming to screeching halts and sudden starts.

Tire Traction

If you are stuck in mud or snow and can't get a push, you might try to get more traction by putting boards or ashes under the tires or by letting some air out of the back tires. Accelerate slowly in low gear so wheels won't spin as fast. Inflate your tires once again as soon as you get to the nearest service station.

If you use chains on your tires to get traction, keep them loose, rather than tight. This provides better traction, and damages your tires the least.

Don't Curb Your Car

Every driver tries to avoid potholes, but not all drivers are that careful about staying away from the curb. When a tire is scraped against a curb the tire fabric is crushed against the rim, snapping the cords in the tire and cutting or scraping the sidewall.

Wheel Alignment and Balance

Tires out of alignment can cut

tire wear by as much as one-half. When tires are out of balance, they'll cause wheels to shimmy and tires to wear unevenly. Even too much play in the steering wheel will take a toll on tires, causing spotty tread wear. Have your wheels aligned and balanced at least once a year by an experienced mechanic. A mechanic who installs too many weights when balancing your wheels may be trying to cover up mistakes he's made. Wheel balancing requires special skill.

Full Gas Tank

When you add gas to your tank, fill it up. A full tank leaves no room for condensation. Condensation adds water to the fuel, which is harmful to the engine.

Proper Lubrication

Keep your car in good condition by following the lubrication advice in your Owner's Manual. Lubricate it regularly, every 1,000-2,000 miles, as indicated. It will pay off in added power, better gas mileage, and longer life for the bearings. Use lightweight oil in cold weather and heavy oil in warmer months. The wrong oil in your car results in wasted gas consumption.

Watch Oil Level

When there is not enough oil circulating in your car, you are doing harm to vital parts. To avoid burned-out bearings, be sure the oil level doesn't fall too low.

Check Wiring Regularly

Do not rely on the attendant who pumps your gas to tell you when the wiring is worn or frayed. Look under the hood yourself regularly and check out the wiring. If you see wiring that appears damaged or defective, make an appointment with a mechanic. In general, wiring should be as far away from hot engine parts as possible. If you notice wiring that seems too close, move it away.

Heater Hose

While you're looking under the hood to check the wiring, take a look at the heater hose. Be sure it's as far away from hot engine parts as possible.

The Fan Belt

If your car's fan belt is too loose or frayed, you may be sure you are wasting gas. On top of that the cylinders may be scored and the battery undercharged as a result. If the fan belt is frayed, get a new one. If the fan belt is too loose, have it tightened.

Temperature Gauge

An engine that's too hot can cause damage to the pistons and cylinder walls as well as other parts. Be sure the cooling system is working properly and check the temperature gauge regularly. The best temperature to operate an engine at is 170-190 degrees Fahrenheit.

Engine Idling

You can add life to your engine if when you park, before turning it off, you allow the engine to idle for a minute or two so that it can cool gradually.

Car Fuses

You can save yourself considerable money and anxiety if you can locate the small box under your dashboard that houses all the fuses for your car. These fuses vary in amperage, and they control your windshield wiper, your signal lights, your radio, your air conditioner and heater, your cigarette lighter, and other accessories.

In your car manual you will find a diagram of the fuse box showing exactly which fuse controns which function.

When you find that one of the above mentioned items is not working, do *not* run to your mechanic before you have checked out the fuse *yourself*. He may charge you $5.00 or $10.00, or more, for correcting what you may possibly be able to correct yourself for not more than 25¢. If it is your windshield wiper that is not working, locate the position of the wiper fuse in the fuse box by checking its location in your Manual. Remove the fuse by simply pulling it out. If it does not come out easily, slide a screwdriver behind and force it out. Don't be afraid to use a bit of pressure. Take the fuse to any store that carries automobile accessories (or to a garage) and purchase an exact duplicate, with the same number of amps. Push into place. If your wiper works, that was your problem. If the wiper still doesn't work, the problem is elsewhere, and your mechanic will have to help you.

Check the Clutch

Be aware of how far you have to push the clutch in when shifting. A clutch that goes in all the way doesn't have much wear left. If the clutch is in good shape, the pedal will have about an inch of play.

A clutch that slips uses more gas than needed, robs the engine of power, and reduces its life-span. Have it relined as soon as possible.

Icy Windshields

To avoid having to scrape hard ice from the windshield of your car on a freezing winter morning, cover the glass with a sheet of vinyl plastic the preceding evening. Place magnets over the vinyl sheet and position them against the metal

windshield molding. In the morning, pull away the plastic, and the windshield will be free of ice.

Cold Weather Care

Keeping a car in a partially heated garage in cold weather will provide the insurance that it won't freeze up. A garage temperature of 40 degrees Fahrenheit is ideal. But whether you garage your car or not, never let the radiator be filled with water only. Anti-freeze should be mixed with the radiator water, and kept in your car throughout the year.

Noisy Doors

To quiet down noisy, squeaky doors, use a can of aerosol oil. Spray it on all hinges. Automotive stores also sell a stick lubricant made especially for quieting squeaky doors.

Stuck Locks

If you can't get your key into the door lock or into the ignition, squeeze powdered graphite into the keyhole, and it should free the lock. If this doesn't work, or if you do not have powdered graphite handy, rub the lead of a soft pencil against the sides of the key. Give the key a good coating and then push it into the lock, moving it in and out a few times before turning. A drop of oil on the key can also be effective in releasing stuck locks.

Frozen Locks

One of the easiest ways to unfreeze a lock is by inserting a hot key. Heat the key with a cigarette lighter or a match. Protect your hands from the heat by wearing gloves, and heat only the tip of the key.

Undercoating

An undercoating will protect the car against rusting caused by spattered road salt and against the spattering of fresh tar-covered gravel. Before you have the job done—which can be expensive— check out

the reliability of the firm that is to do the work. Many outfits promise more than they deliver, and you can hardly check for yourself whether the job has been done properly.

Shellacking Chrome

The chrome on your car will stay bright indefinitely if you protect it with shellac. Apply one or two thin coats of fresh white shellac every six months.

Surface Rusting

Wax improves a car's appearance, and it also protects the surface against rusting and fading. Wax the car right after you've washed and dried it.

Gas Cap Holder

If you have ever lost your gas cap because you or the gas station attendant forgot to replace it after filling your tank, you might want to avoid that unpleasant experience from happening again. You can if

you attach a small magnet to the inside of the small door which closes over the gas-tank opening. The magnet will hold the cap while the tank is being filled. In this way the cap cannot be misplaced and the door cannot be closed until the cap is screwed back in place.

Remove Bugs

To remove insects squashed against the hood of the car, use linen or nylon net dampened in water. Without scratching the surface, the fibers will act as a mild abrasive.

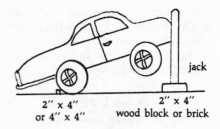

jack

2" x 4"
or 4" x 4"

2" x 4"
wood block or brick

Radio Antennas

Radio antennas often get pitted by weather and become difficult to move. You can avoid this difficulty by rubbing a coat of wax on them, especially in winter.

Car Jacks

Since cars have to be jacked up quite a distance to change tires, you can take some of the strain off the jack by putting it on a platform made from two-by-fours or four-by-fours. This will raise the jack sufficiently to avoid the arching that often occurs when the jack is raised. You will also find that the car will stand more firmly with a platform under the jack.

Don't get under the car while it is in a raised position. Also, place short two-by-fours, or bricks, under the wheels that are not being raised, to prevent the car from rolling.

Dashboard Coin-holder

A small metal box attached to the dashboard of your car can be a very convenient place to keep coins for tolls and small purchases. Instead of drilling holes and attaching the box with sheet metal screws, use a magnet to hold the box in place.

Oil Can Covers

The plastic lid from a one-pound can of coffee will fit perfectly over a one-quart can of motor oil.

Key Holder

Place a spare set of your car keys in a tightly-closed, small metal box and put a powerful magnet on the box. Place the magnet and box somewhere under the car where it cannot be detected easily. Then, if you misplace the original set, you will have a spare set handy.

Stain-free Garages

To keep garage floors free of oil stains, place a pan of sand on the spot where the oil drips, and leave it there. Wood shavings will work as well. Clean the pan, or add more sand or wood from time to time.

Precautions When Buying Used Cars

When buying a used car, you should spend the money and have a mechanic look it over. But before doing that, here are a few tests you can do yourself.

1. Test the shocks by pushing down on each bumper in turn. Note whether the car levels off quickly without bouncing.

2. Check the oil. Remove the dipstick. If the oil clings to it, it may indicate that the seller has added a very heavy oil to cover up a defective engine.

3. Most engines sound good once they finally get started, so pay special attention to the sound of the motor when you *first* start it. If it sounds peculiar, beware!

4. At a cruising speed of around 25 miles per hour, push the accelerator to the floor. A sound engine will quickly and steadily pick up speed.

5. Be aware of how the shift feels when you take off on your test drive, and how it feels after you've been on the road for a while. Some dealers attempt to silence a noisy transmission—with oatmeal or bananas.

6. Test-drive the car in uncongested traffic. At 35 miles per hour, take your hands off the steering wheel. The car should steer itself straight for about 50 yards. Also, be sure there is sufficient play in the steering wheel. You should be able to turn the steering wheel about 1½ inches before the front wheels start to move.

7. Test-drive the car over some bumps. If the suspension is in good shape, the car should take the bumps smoothly and quietly.

8. Check the automatic drive for proper acceleration on an average uphill grade. There should be no slippage. Then, back the car up a short hill. It should make the climb smoothly.

9. When applying the brakes suddenly, the car should not pull to one side. The brakes need some work if it does.

10. Get all promises and guarantees *in writing*. They should be indicated on the bill of sale and should be signed by the owner (or dealer).

11. If you are purchasing a used car on the installment plan, be sure to get an itemized accounting of the cost, including down payment, monthly payments, interest charges, and any additional charges. Check carefully before signing the agreement.

Chapter Ten

MISCELLANEOUS HINTS AND TIPS

The Person-to-Person Call

It may slip your mind when you are in a hurry, but money can be saved on long-distance calls. If you suspect the party you want to talk with is *not* at home, call person-to-person. The call will cost nothing. If you call station-to-station and someone answers, you'll be charged whether the party you want is in or not.

Long-distance Telephone Calls

The cost of a long-distance telephone call depends on how long you talk. You can talk less and still get your information across if you jot down ahead of time the topics you want to cover. But an even greater saving will be yours if you check with your telephone company and become aware of the hours when the rates are cheapest. Usually, night rates and holiday rates are least expensive.

Telephone Savings

If you want to cut down on your long-distance charges, time your own calls. Keep an hourglass egg

timer next to the phone, and it will let you know when those first three minutes are up.

Wooden Handles

Wooden handles that attach to brushes and brooms are worthless when their threads are spent. But you can add new life to them if you will wrap the worn threads with one or more turns of adhesive tape. Twist the handle back into the socket and the fit will be secure again. If the brush is still loose, add another turn of tape.

Seeing Around Corners

A bicycle mirror secured to a flashlight will direct the beam of light at an angle and reflect the area at which the light is directed. The "flashlight that can see around corners" comes in handy when working on an automobile or installing plumbing.

Umbrella Stands

When an umbrella stand gathers the drippings from wet umbrellas, the dampness pervades the room, and the deep bottom is very difficult to dry out. One way of keeping a pool of water from sitting on the bottom for days on end is to line it with a sponge cut to size. Squeeze the sponge dry from time to time.

Key Handles

Don't throw away old toothbrushes. If it does not already have one, drill a hole at the end opposite the brush. Cut away the brush and round off the edges with a file. Secure your key or keys to it with ring or a twist of wire or an old shower-curtain hook, and hang it on a wall so it is readily available. To identify it in the future, mark the handle with a marking pencil and cover it with cellophane tape.

Stubborn Zippers

Stuck zippers often need no more than a dab of silicone lubricant to loosen them. It is the same lubricant you would use to eliminate squeaks from doors, and is available at hardware stores. Squirt some of the lubricant on your finger, then rub it into the zipper.

Leftover Wallpaper

Leftover wallpaper can be used to decorate some of the accessories in the same room. Remnants can be used to cover a wastebasket, a tissue box holder, or a window shade.

Used Flashlight Cases

A worn-out, metal flashlight case makes a handy container for pencils, pens, rulers and tools—especially cases with magnetic holders, which can be attached to metal filing cabinets, kitchen cabinets or refrigerators. If the tube is too deep, stuff cotton or paper in the bottom.

Label Protection

If you want to be sure the label you have written to mail a package will not become smeared, rub a candle over the writing. The wax will form a weatherproof coating.

Envelope Sealant

Dab a little nail polish on the flap of a non-sticking envelope. It will dry fast and not leave a smudge. The seal will be so secure that even steam will not be able to open it.

Anti-fraying Knots

To keep knots from untying and

the ends of rope from fraying, use shellac. Dip the ends or apply the shellac with a brush or cloth. Allow to dry for 30 minutes before using.

Sharpening Scissors

A quick way to sharpen scissors that are not overly dull, but can stand a bit of honing, is to make about six cuts into a piece of fine sandpaper. Scissors with very dull cutting edges require a regular sharpening.

Rusty Scissors

It's not a good idea to use sandpaper or steel wool for removing rust from scissors. To remove rust use household ammonia. Put ammonia on the rusty spots and let it soak in for several minutes. Then, wipe off the rust with a soft cloth.

Cutting Foam Rubber

Foam rubber doesn't cut easily, unless you compress it. Press against the foam rubber with a flat board or a book, and use a sharp, long-bladed knife for cutting. If the knife grabs against the foam rubber, lubricate the blade by dipping it in water.

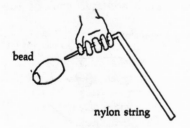

bead

nylon string

Stringing Beads

Stringing beads without the use of a needle is not difficult if you use the right kind of string. Nylon fishing line is ideal for the purpose—it is strong, flexible, and stiff enough not to require a needle. Dental floss is good too. Dip one end in nail polish. After it dries the end will be firm enough to use as a needle.

Soundproof Clock

If the sound of a ticking clock is disturbing, cover the clock with a large glass tumbler, a jar, or a bowl.

Storing Christmas Ornaments

Egg cartons make good places for storing Christmas ornaments, especially the styrofoam cartons. For larger ornaments, cut the tops of two boxes off and place the bottoms together. Secure them with rubber bands or string. The lids can be used for storing odd-shaped decorations or candles. Tubes from rolls of paper towels or toilet tissue are likewise useful in storing candles and small electric bulbs. Stuff the bottom with paper first, and label each tube.

Deodorizing the Sickroom

Vinegar will deodorize a sickroom if a few drops are sprinkled along the baseboard on all sides of the room.

Battery Corrosion

Ordinary carbon-zinc batteries will cause corrosion in your flashlight if they remain in the case for any length of time after they are "burned out." Remove batteries from the case if you do not use your flashlight frequently, and put them back only when you are planning to

flash light   cover   batteries

use it. The alkaline type battery will last the longest.

Propane Lamps

When the electric power fails and remains off for a considerable length of time, one of the best and safest emergency lights is the pro-

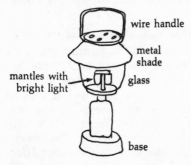

wire handle

metal shade

mantles with bright light

glass

base

pane lamp. It provides a brilliant light and its fuel—propane—can be stored safely in its sealed steel cylinders without deteriorating. Although gasoline lanterns also provide brilliant light, gasoline deteriorates with age and is difficult to store safely.

Emergency Stoves I

Keep a propane camp stove along with some fuel cylinders in a handy

camp stove

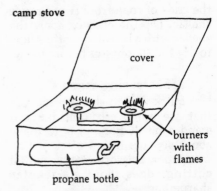

cover

burners with flames

propane bottle

place in your cellar for those emergency situations when the electric power goes out for more than a few hours and you can't cook on your electric range. A propane camp stove can do everything that can be done on a bottled gas stove. The fuel is the same, the only difference is that the camp stove has room for only two pots.

Emergency Stoves II

If you have an electric stove, be prepared for a power failure emergency, by having a Sterno-type stove handy. They are inexpensive, easy to store because they fold flat and their solid alcohol-type fuel, that is safely stored in cans, burns with a clean blue flame. With a two-pot Sterno and two cans of fuel,

metal sterno stove

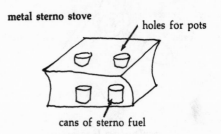

holes for pots

cans of sterno fuel

you can easily cook a meal for four people in 1½ hours.

Window Security I

One-way screws are recommended for locks on windows and doors with glass panes. By breaking or cutting the glass, a burglar can reach in with a screwdriver and turn the ordinary screws that fasten a window or door lock. On a one-way screw the top left and lower right quarters on either side of the slot are missing. This makes it possible to turn it from left to right when screwing it in, but im-

raised

possible to turn from right to left to unscrew it.

Window Security II

In addition to the normal window lock on all windows, you may want extra protection for windows burglars may use as entry points. Drill a hole through the upper and lower halves of a window that will accommodate a nail at least three inches long. Select a drill that is the same diameter as the nail to be inserted.

Security During Vacations I

Homes that have a lived-in look are rarely troubled by burglars. If

you are going to be away for a while, leave a key with a trustworthy neighbor. Ask the neighbor to remove mail from your mail box daily and remove circulars and debris from the walk. Also ask the neighbor to vary the positions of your drapes and blinds daily.

Security During Vacations II

Arrange to have somebody cut your lawn while you are away on vacation. Make sure deliveries of newspapers and milk are not made in your absence. Put at least one outside light and one or more interior lights on electric timers so that they go on at night. You may want to let your local police department know you will be away so they can check your house regularly.

Storing Inflammable Liquids

When you store an inflammable product, make sure it's kept in a metal container. Fuels and solvents stored in glass containers may expand during a heat wave, and explode. If a spark or flame is present when this occurs, fire will result. Whatever the metal container you use, make sure the lid is on tightly.

Preparing for Winter

Prepare for winter immediately after Thanksgiving.

1. Remove screens and store them flat. If they need repair or painting, this is the time to do it.
2. Clean window frames and door frames before fitting storm doors and windows. If caulking is needed around the frames, do it.
3. Insulate any exposed plumbing pipes that are likely to freeze.

Christmas Tree Fires

Many fires are caused because Christmas trees are dry and brittle, and catch fire easily. A simple way of minimizing chances of accidental fire in your home is to observe the following suggestions:

1. Always purchase a *fresh* tree.
2. Always store your tree in a cool place, and keep its base in a container of water.
3. Always make a fresh cut in the base of your tree (as soon as you bring it home). Your cut should be about one inch from the old one. The fresh cut will allow the tree to absorb water more easily.
4. Always keep lukewarm water in the container that is holding the tree. Warm water is absorbed by the tree more easily than cold water.